Writing
Quebec

SELECTED ESSAYS BY
HUBERT AQUIN

Writing Quebec

EDITED, WITH AN INTRODUCTION, BY
ANTHONY PURDY

Translated from the French by
Paul Gibson, Reva Joshee,
Anthony Purdy and Larry Shouldice

 THE UNIVERSITY OF ALBERTA PRESS

First published by
The University of Alberta Press
Athabasca Hall
Edmonton, Alberta
Canada T6G 2E8

Copyright © The University of Alberta Press 1988

Canadian Cataloguing in Publication Data

Aquin, Hubert, 1929–1977.
Writing Quebec : selected essays

Includes bibliographical references.
ISBN 0–88864–130–3 (bound). —
ISBN 0–88864–131–1 (pbk.)

1. Canadian literature (French) - 20th century -
History and criticism.* 2. Canadian literature
(French) - Quebec (Province) - History and
criticism.* I. Purdy, Anthony George, 1949-
II. Title.
PS8501.Q85A25 1988   C844'. 54 C88–091169–7
PQ3919.A65A25 1988

"The Cultural Fatigue of French Canada," translated by Larry
Shouldice, in *Contemporary Quebec Criticism*, edited and translated by Larry Shouldice (Toronto. University of Toronto Press,
1979) is reprinted with permission of University of Toronto Press.

Frontispiece by Kèro.

Typesetting by The Typeworks, Vancouver, British Columbia
Printed by Hignell Printing Ltd., Winnipeg, Manitoba, Canada

CONTENTS

PREFACE

The essays collected here were written over a period of some fifteen years from 1961 to 1976. Most of them first appeared in journals, newspapers and magazines such as *Liberté*, *Parti pris*, *Mosaic*, *Maintenant*, *Cul Q*, *Le Devoir* and *Mainmise*. Original publication details for the French texts are given with each essay. One of the essays, "Occupation: Writer," was reprinted in Hubert Aquin, *Point de fuite* (Montreal: Cercle du Livre de France, 1971), pp. 47–59. All the other texts were collected and presented by René Lapierre in Hubert Aquin, *Blocs erratiques* (Montreal: Quinze, Collection "Prose entière," 1977). Larry Shouldice's translation of "The Cultural Fatigue of French Canada" originally appeared in *Contemporary Quebec Criticism*, edited and translated by Larry Shouldice (Toronto: The University of Toronto Press, 1979). It is reprinted by permission of University of Toronto Press with minor revisions.

The essays selected are intended to give a fairly representative picture of Aquin's mature thought as it ranges through a variety of subjects, mixing disciplines and approaches with disconcerting ease, moving mischievously from politics to mysticism, from history to mathematics in an endless provocation of the reader. There are, however, constants; whether he is talking about language or literature, separatism or colonialism, Aquin never loses sight of an overriding concern which haunts and informs everything he writes: the question of Quebec's national identity as a political, cultural and historical reality. It is within this general preoccupation that Aquin situates the perpetual, nagging predicament of the Quebec writer, who must constantly ask himself not only how to write in Quebec, but how to write Quebec, how to come to terms in his writing with the ambiguities, the dilemmas, and the powerful and frequently destructive emotions that his situation entails. Hence the title of this collection, which reflects not simply a literary problem, but an ontological one: for Aquin, Quebec has to write itself into being, has to learn how to tell its own story; anything less is simply compensation for a lived historical and political impotence.

The present volume has not been conceived as a scholarly edition, but rather as an introduction, for the student or general reader interested in the literature, politics and history of French Canada, to the thought of one of Quebec's leading novelists and thinkers of the nineteen-sixties and seventies. Notes have therefore been kept to a minimum and are used either to give pertinent details concerning an essay's provenance or to remind readers of historical and biographical facts they may have forgotten. Thus, while the reader can be expected to know, or find out for himself, that the Apostle of Patmos refers to St. John of the *Apocalypse*, it seems less likely that the average reader will recall the role of Charles Hindenlang in the events of 1838 or that Maurice Lamontagne was a member of the Pearson cabinet from 1963 to 1965. No protocol will please every reader; suffice it to say that the objective throughout has been to facilitate the understanding of the text while intruding as little as possible.

With the exception of "The Cultural Fatigue of French Canada," all the essays have been translated by Paul Gibson, Reva Joshee and myself. My thanks go to my co-translators for their cooperation and patience, and to the Canada Council for providing a translation grant. Thanks, too, to Marie Greenslade for her help with the notes, to Larry

Shouldice and the University of Toronto Press for permission to reprint "The Cultural Fatigue of French Canada," and to Gordon Sheppard who read an early version of several of the essays. Henri Tuchmaïer, at the University of Western Ontario, first introduced me to Aquin's work some twelve years ago and must be eternally thanked, as must my students at the University of Alberta, who have kept alive my belief that Aquin has something of vital importance to say to all Canadians who are concerned about the past, present and future of their country. I am grateful, too, to the director of the University of Alberta Press, Norma Gutteridge, who has encouraged this project since its conception, and to my editor, Mary Mahoney-Robson, whose enthusiasm and efficiency make her a delight to work with. I also wish to thank Kèro Beaudoin for providing the photographs of Aquin. Finally, my deepest thanks go to Emmanuel Aquin and Andrée Yanacopoulo for permission to translate the essays. Madame Yanacopoulo has been particularly helpful and encouraging over a period of some three years since I first contacted her. This volume is dedicated to her.

INTRODUCTION

Hubert Aquin committed suicide in March 1977, a matter of months after the Parti Québécois came to power. Today, the euphoria of November '76 and the polarized emotions of the 1980 Referendum, which signalled the end of Quebec's love affair with independence, seem like distant memories. There is once again a Liberal government in Quebec headed by the man René Lévesque defeated all those years ago, and I am writing these words in the wake of the Meech Lake accord, which alters the balance of power between the federal and provincial governments and brings Quebec into the Constitution under, more or less, its own terms, despite the protests of Aquin's old adversary, Pierre Trudeau. In Ottawa, the War Measures Act, last invoked by Trudeau in 1970 during the FLQ crisis, is under review, though it is not at all clear that the recommended changes will make for a more civilized piece of legislation. The Government's proposed new Official Languages Act, which would allow the Secretary of State to promote actively the rights of official language minorities, is under serious fire from the Tories' own backbenchers. Meanwhile, here in Edmonton where I write, a French-speaking MLA who tried to ask a question (about French-language education) in his own language in the Alberta legislature was ordered by a committee of the legislature to apologize for his behaviour; the same committee recommended that the *Edmonton Journal* be admonished for questioning the Speaker's judgment in refusing to allow the question.

My intention is not to dwell on the ironies of political life, or indeed to comment on the increasingly conservative mood of the late nineteen-eighties at a time when support for the incumbent federal Progressive Conservative Party is paradoxically low. After all, by the time this book is published these trends may well have been reversed. My concern is rather to show that, despite spectacular swings in public mood and far-reaching changes in governments and policies, the problems and concerns raised by Aquin in many of the essays which make up this volume are still acutely relevant to Quebec and to Canada today. Indeed, as most of those problems concern the fundamental question of what, historically, culturally and politically, constitutes national identity, it is not likely that they can be wished or legislated out of existence. They are part of the reality of Canada; they will not go away.

Aquin's great merit was to have looked these problems in the face and to have told his fellow Québécois, with all the passion he felt and all the lucidity which characterized his thought, what he saw there. The picture he drew is not reassuring and the remedies he proposed are neither comfortable nor consistent, varying from essay to essay as his own mood shifted in response to changing circumstances. But what Aquin can tell the English-speaking reader of today is what it means, intellectually and emotionally, to be a minority in a country of minorities, what it feels like to be prey to a host of conflicting emotions concerning one's own most intimate identity as defined by and in one's language. Whether or not we share Aquin's political goals and prejudices (and he is the first to own up to them), it is a lesson we should learn and learn well for the sake of all our futures.

Hubert Aquin is best known as the author of four novels, all of which have been translated, published between 1965 and 1974.[1] What is less well known outside Quebec is the volume and diversity of Aquin's output as a creative writer and journalist. From his beginnings in the late nineteen-forties to his death in 1977, Aquin produced hundreds of essays, articles, short stories, translations, plays, adaptations, scripts for radio, television and film, as well as numerous pieces of an occasional nature.[2] Some of the shorter texts have been collected in *Point de fuite* (1971) and *Blocs erratiques* (1977). It should soon be possible to gauge more accurately the scope and importance of Aquin's work and his influence on the literary and cultural life of Quebec, as the first volume of an ambitious critical edition of his works, which has been underway for a number of years now, is scheduled to appear in 1988–89.[3]

The essays translated here span the period from 1961 to 1976, from the early years of the Quiet Revolution to the election of the Parti Québécois. They were written at a time of strong nationalist sentiment, a time of rapid and turbulent change which affected every aspect of life in Quebec. As such, they represent one man's attempt to understand those changes and to give positive direction to the intellectual and emotional energy which was released by the events of his time. The essays are presented here chronologically, an order I will generally respect in these introductory remarks. Other arrangements would certainly have been possible, along thematic or stylistic lines, but the relations within and between groups of essays would then become so complex as to blur the evolution of Aquin's thought. I have chosen, then, to talk about the relations within a context of change rather than try to systematize Aquin's thought at the expense of history.

The first four essays were published in 1961–62 in *Liberté*, a journal which was founded in 1959 (the year of Duplessis' death) and which heralded in many ways the end of Quebec's Great Darkness and the start of the banquet years of the sixties. Aquin, who was associated with the journal for a number of years, served briefly as editor in 1961–62 and the first text, "Dangerous Understanding," is an example of his editorial style. Apart from the dramatic call for change, three things stand out in this brief piece. Firstly, that the ideology of French Canada is not reducible to its social institutions—whether they be political, religious or educational—but is rather to be seen as a "collective unconscious, the protean product of two centuries of repressed desire." The notion of a collective French-Canadian unconscious dating back to the traumatic events of the Conquest is one that Aquin will never aban-

don and that will colour everything he writes. This stress on the unconscious elements of the French-Canadian psyche brings us to the second
important feature of the essay: the insistence on the necessity of understanding, of not being simply swept along by the tide of events. This is a
refrain which will be heard frequently in the essays of this period, particularly in "The Politics of Existence" and "The Cultural Fatigue of
French Canada," where it will take the form of a praise of dialectic in
an attempt to outreason Pierre Trudeau on the question of nationalism.
The third aspect of "Dangerous Understanding" which we should bear
in mind for future consideration is the affirmation of the value of language as a mode of action. While his position on the question will become considerably more ambiguous in future texts, the general problem of language will never be far from Aquin's mind as he struggles in
his essays and fiction with a collective identity crisis in which language
plays a determining role.

Language figures prominently in the next essay, "Form and (Dis-)
content," where Aquin draws an analogy between happiness (as a passive, counter-revolutionary attitude to life) and felicity of style. (The
French title, "Le bonheur d'expression," plays on this double sense of
happiness, creating an ambiguity I have tried to maintain in my translation.) According to Aquin, artists are "professionals of unhappiness"
who, far from seeing art as a form of compensation, use their gifts to
express their dissatisfaction and give form to their discontent. For a
more concrete idea of what this *malheur d'expression*, this deliberately
chosen infelicity of style, entails, we shall have to wait for the much
more flamboyant, "terrorist" texts of 1964–65. What should be re-
tained from the 1961 essay is the strong emphasis placed by Aquin on
style itself. Not content with Buffon's "Style is the man," Aquin goes an
important step further to suggest that style is the manifestation of the
collective unconscious in and through the individual artist. Once again,
this is an idea which will have great currency throughout the essays
and the fiction, though with changing emphasis.

Published in March 1962, "The Politics of Existence" is perhaps
Aquin's most explicitly political essay, dealing as it does with the nuts
and bolts of his nationalism. (At the time, he was heavily involved with
the Rassemblement pour l'Indépendance Nationale (RIN) for which he
would serve as vice-president for the Montreal region in 1964.) Within
the separatist position from which it speaks, the article gives a remarkably lucid and balanced account of the inconsistencies characterizing

both the various independence movements of the day and the opposition to them. Aquin's message is simple: if French Canadians are serious about their nationalism, it is time for them to pass from an emotional refusal of minority status and of English domination (a refusal which has played an important part in the *historical* development of separatism) to the concrete *political* struggle for independence, which will be fought not against English Canadians but against French Canadians. Or, in the religious terms which Aquin finds appropriate to the subject of nationalism, it is time to pass from faith to works, from sermons on the mount to properly articulated policies, which means taking a stand on the major political issues which divide French Canada. (It is worth pointing out that the revolution of which Aquin speaks in this text has nothing to do with the violent overthrow of elected government, an option which is specifically rejected; Aquin is thinking rather of a political and social revolution to be accomplished through the electoral struggle and parliamentary process. His position in this respect will not always be so clear.)

Equally important in "The Politics of Existence" are the emphasis on nationalism as a matter of political will and the belief, derived from Sartrean existentialism, that a people is defined by its project rather than by its past. Both of these ideas are taken up in Aquin's longest and most important essay of the period, "The Cultural Fatigue of French Canada," where he writes that nations and peoples have no essence, that they are "ontologically indeterminate, and this indetermination is the very foundation of their freedom." Conceived as a response to an anti-nationalist article published in *Cité Libre* by Pierre Elliott Trudeau, Aquin's essay starts with an eloquent plea for reason to prevail in the discussion of emotional issues such as nationalism, war and the atomic bomb. The arguments are too rich and varied to summarize adequately here, so I shall simply attempt to pick out a few of the main strands which seem to me to be important for an understanding of Aquin's thought in general.

The first of these strands is the concept of cultural fatigue itself, a notion which links with the idea of a French-Canadian collective unconscious. Cultural fatigue is a kind of collective guilt-complex, a psychological state induced by an awareness of belonging to a colonized minority; it is characterized by a sense of dispossession which takes the form of "self-punishment, masochism, a sense of unworthiness, 'depression,' the lack of enthusiasm and vigour." Its manifestations are treated with paternalistic tolerance by the majority as "a form of adolescent impulsiveness" which can be transformed into a rite of passage, a "kind of cathartic melodrama." Thus, the "system" in no way implies the disappearance of the French fact in Canada: "it means simply that this French fact must be domesticated at all levels and in every conscience." The full force of Aquin's scorn is reserved in this respect for Trudeau and like-minded thinkers who try to shift the collective, political problem to the individual, psychological level by claiming that all that is required to remedy the situation is for French Canadians to be individually better, to make themselves indispensable to the destiny of their masters. (This is essentially the same argument we hear today about the unemployed—there is no unemployment problem, only lazy people—and about women's issues: of course women can compete in a man's world—they just have to have the right attitude.)

It is in this context that Aquin, playing on the double meaning of the French word *histoire*, introduces the key concept of history as story: "In this scenario, French Canada would play a role, sometimes even a starring role, in a story it could never write itself." Such a view of French-Canadian history as script or story contains a clear allusion to Lord Durham's infamous statement of 1839 to the effect that French Canadians are a people without literature and without history. Indeed, says Aquin, Durham was right: "History obviously belonged to English Canadians, and all we could do was to take it as one takes a train." If French Canada has no history, it is because it suffers from a chronic disability to tell its own story, a theme which will be of central importance a few years later in "The Art of Defeat" as well as in Aquin's first novel, *Prochain Épisode*.

History belongs, then, by virtue of an initial act of Conquest, to English Canada, and Aquin will insist, throughout the early essays, on the historical necessity of defining French Canada in relation to its (unequal) partner in Confederation. In this respect, Aquin's consistent use during this period of the term *French Canada* rather than *Quebec* perhaps requires a word of explanation. In the first place, it should be pointed out that the designation *French Canada* in no way compromises Aquin's separatist position; indeed, it is essential to his formulation of the historical problem and is closely connected to his conception of dialectic fatigue. I have already pointed out Aquin's insistence on the need for true thought or dialectic, which alone can prevent conflict from degenerating into a dialogue of the deaf as both sides retreat into their preconceived systems and their party lines. In particular, dialectic is seen as a guarantee against the temptations of a facile causality. It is on these grounds that Aquin attacks Trudeau's attempts to establish an invariable causal link between nationalism and war, complaining that such an argument leads to a doctrine of transcendent pacifism which has the effect of blocking all serious thought on the questions involved. According to Aquin, Trudeau's anti-nationalism is dangerous precisely in that it refuses to recognize that, historically, Canada is the site of a dialectical confrontation between two cultures. Instead, the dialectic is displaced by shifting the context of definition and over-valuing the higher term of reference, saying that "French Canada is very small compared to reality X... and its totality becomes simply a particularity in this new scale of size." The French Canadian's nationalist aspirations are thus easily crushed by placing them in "dialectical" opposition to any number of transcendent terms, of which nuclear warfare is merely the most dramatic and all-embracing. Similarly, the dialectical reality of the two Canadian cultures is denied by placing it in the political context of federal-provincial relations: "The federal superstructure, in sanctifying the political appeasement of French Canada, does not stem from the historical dialectic of the two Canadas, but from a desire to suppress this dialectic, so that Ottawa, a capital between two provinces, rules over ten of them. The political portrait of Canada masks the real confrontation between two cultures and glosses over this confrontation in a disguised monolithic regime which legalistically considers French Canada to be one province in ten."

The particular weight attributed to the term *French Canada* in Aquin's usage should now be clear. Whereas Quebec is the name of a political entity defined by its (minority) position within Confederation, French Canada represents a cultural group which defines itself historically in relation to another cultural group—that of English Canada. For Aquin, to realize the Canadian dialectic is to work toward the politicization of that historical confrontation. By the same token, to confine French Canada to the province of Quebec is to depoliticize the notion of culture, reducing it to its least offensive, "regionalist" manifestations. The whole problem of terminology can be thrown into stark relief by asking what the effects would be of changing the essay's title from "The Cultural Fatigue of French Canada" to "The Cultural Fatigue of Quebec." Clearly, a very large part of the argument would simply disappear. Paradoxically, in 1987, after the Referendum and after the eclipse of the Parti Québécois, the "cultural fatigue of Quebec" is perhaps a much more meaningful expression than it would have been in 1962.

"Occupation: Writer" marks a shift to a more revolutionary stance and style. Published in *Parti pris*, a journal with a strong Marxist emphasis and a nationalist ideology of decolonization derived from thinkers like Memmi, Fanon, Senghor and Césaire, the essay returns to the notion of style discussed in "Form and (Dis-)content" and places it in the context of a Quebec rocked by the first round of FLQ bombings. "In this flaming bordello of a country in pieces," declaims Aquin, "writing is like saying one's prayers while sitting on a nitroglycerine bomb set to explode in five minutes time." What follows is an impassioned analysis of the role of the writer or the artist in a minority culture. According to Aquin, colonized countries or minority groups invariably produce excessive quantities of art and literature: "For want of realities, there is an overproduction of symbols." Here again we find the idea of a collective unconscious taken up in conjunction with the concept of history as a story told by others: "Yes, to be dominated is to live a novel written in advance, to conform unconsciously to patterns of behaviour which are sufficiently ambiguous for their meaning to escape those who are caught up in them." In such a society, art is inevitably seen as a compensation for the lack of any real power, undergoing in the process a kind of folklorization: "The domination of one human group by another places an exaggerated importance on those powers of the inferior group which are harmless: sex, artistic proclivities, natural talent for music or creation, and so on. Are we not, as French Canadians, interested in Eskimo art and in the mythology of the Indians we keep on reservations?"

Aquin's initial reaction is to refuse to write, to refuse a talent which testifies only to his minority status and conditioning as a member of a dominated group: "In rejecting domination I refuse literature, the daily bread of the dominated." But is Aquin's refusal as total as it would at first appear? In fact, we soon notice that the argument slips from an outright refusal to write to a more qualified rejection of what he calls "literature": that is, writing which operates within the all-too-coherent system of compensation characteristic of paternalistic colonialism. The solution apparently lies in a kind of terrorist writing, which steps outside the dialogue binding dominator and dominated and opts for incoherence, monologue and madness.

Does this mean that Aquin is a committed writer in the Sartrean sense? In fact, it is a term he dislikes, refusing any narrow interpretation of political commitment in art in the same breath as he denounces the head-in-the-sand view of literature as an inner adventure: "No writer is required to toe the literary line laid down according to the options of a particular political system, any more than he is committed by his wordmongering to take a vow of historical chastity and renounce all but the production of a posthumous and autarkical work of art." To the narrowly political imperative of commitment (*engagement*), Aquin prefers the broader cultural one of *enracinement*, of writing out of one's roots: "One does not choose one's native land; still, it is better to put down roots and take nourishment, symbiotically, from this cold earth we have trodden since childhood." This does not, however, mean falling into the trap of folklorization, of using one's country for romantic local colour, thereby collaborating in the depoliticization of culture; on the contrary, it means finding a style which expresses the reality of the society in which one lives. In Aquin's case, it means coming to terms in writing with the ontological turmoil of Quebec; it means inventing the forms which correspond to and illuminate the disarray of his people: "Syntax, form, the meaning of words—all are subject to explosion. In a country which is blacking out, the writer who attempts to breathe life into what is killing him will not write a Stendhalian tale of French-Canadian *carbonari*, but a work as uncertain and formally unwholesome as the one taking place in him and in his country." This, then, is the *malheur d'expression* announced in 1961, the style capable of conveying the unhappiness not just of an artist but of a dispossessed and alienated people: "It is a waste of time to write novels unsullied by the intolerable realities of our collective daily life, in an antiseptic French untouched by the spasms which shake the ground we walk on."

Aquin's own monologue, his attempt to break with the compensatory and therapeutic structures of literature in order to give full voice to the passion and daily agony of French Canada's "difficulty of being," was to be written later that year. *Prochain Épisode*, Aquin's first novel, was written in the Institut Prévost, a Montreal psychiatric clinic where he was held while awaiting trial on a weapons charge, on which he was subsequently acquitted. In many ways the novel can be seen as a fictional working through of the problems outlined in the dismissive self-portrait offered in "Occupation: Writer": "The good little French Canadian, destined for a brilliant if frivolous future, suddenly takes it upon himself to produce a piece of writing governed by the thematics of the refusal to write—a meaningless gesture which might acquire significance only by the simultaneous explosion of all the sticks of dynamite which now lie rotting in the arsenals of the Province of Quebec." *Prochain Épisode* was not, then, written simply to "pass the time" during Aquin's confinement. Contrary to what the myth would have us believe, there is nothing contingent or anecdotal about the genesis of the novel, which grows out of some of the main ideas expressed in the essays published between 1961 and 1964. The refusal to write might be seen in retrospect as a kind of rhetorical stance which masks a less dramatic if more productive quest for the kind of literature that might be possible in Quebec. In this respect, *Prochain Épisode* is neither a revolutionary novel (in the sense that it sets out to portray a revolutionary episode) nor, as certain critics have claimed, a counter-revolutionary novel (in the sense that it portrays the inevitable failure and recuperation of revolutionary activity). It is rather, as its title would indicate, a *pre*-revolutionary novel—a novel which, while exorcizing the myths and compensatory temptations of a colonized people, presents a lucid analysis of cultural fatigue and its historical determinants.

Three other essays were published in 1964–65. While not as verbally flamboyant as "Occupation: Writer," each of them develops a central image or conceit with a certain revolutionary brio. "The Mystic Body" is a lighthearted deconstruction of the journalistic and political rhetoric of love, marriage and sex used to describe the cohabitation of two nations in Confederation. Quebec, of course, is the woman in these macho metaphors—and this indirectly raises a very interesting point. For if nationalism in its various manifestations was the source of the most vibrant and characteristic political and cultural discourse of Quebec in the nineteen-sixties and early seventies, that honour has undoubtedly fallen in the intervening years to feminism. And one of the reasons that Quebec feminism has been such a dominant cultural force is that many of the structures and strategies of analysis and subversion that it has adopted were already in place in the cultural community in the discourse of nationalism, as developed in the pages of journals like *Parti pris*. (A clear idea of just how smooth the transposition is can be had by imagining the application of the analysis of cultural fatigue and its psychological corollaries to the case of the battered wife—an image which, interestingly enough, does not appear as such in "The Mystic Body.")

"The Differential Calculus of Counter-Revolution" continues in the same light vein as Aquin attempts to formulate the dynamics and the psychology of counter-revolution in terms of a mathematical theorem. Once again we are struck by Aquin's enormous pleasure in language and the sheer verbal energy which characterizes his imagination. On a more serious note, "The Art of Defeat" brings us back to a historical event which never ceased to haunt Aquin: the rebellion of 1837–38. But here again, as the sub-title—"A Matter of Style"—indicates, Aquin returns to one of his favourite metaphors, indulging, in the middle of a Maoist analysis of the guerilla tactics that the *Patriotes* failed to adopt, in a curious parenthetical meditation on why, in the opening battle at St. Denis, the rebels failed to take advantage of their victory and rout the English troops. It is like being at a performance of a classical tragedy, suggests Aquin, in which the entire chorus suddenly forgets its lines. Or perhaps there is another explanation for the uneasy silence: "The chorus, dumbstruck, cannot say its lines if what has just happened on stage was not in the script; the *Patriotes* did not forget their lines at St. Denis, but were thrown by an event which was not part of the play: their own victory!" History, we recall, belongs to English Canada, and the *Patriotes*, like all good French Canadians, are incapable of improvising their *own* story. The defeat at St. Denis is above all a narrative defeat, a failure of the will to history. The narrative impotence of the rebels of 1837 will be transposed into the hesitations of the autobiographical narrator of *Prochain Épisode* and his inability to narrate the death of his hero's enemy, the historian H. de Heutz.[4]

The three essays written in 1968–69 all deal with the question of the writer and his relationship with society. "Literature and Alienation" and "Thoughts on the Status of the Writer" are both straightforward pieces which affirm, each in its own way, the freedom of the writer to experiment and find his own mode of expression. "The Death of the Accursed Writer" is a more lively—if somewhat incoherent—piece which continues in the same anti-romantic, Joycean vein, calling for such sacred notions as spontaneity and inspiration to be abandoned and replaced with a new respect for the artist as craftsman. But the accursed writer—the term recalls the *poètes maudits*: Baudelaire, Rimbaud, Verlaine—is not dead; in the Quebec of 1969 he is "simply the embodiment of the ambiguous vocation of the people of Quebec." In this sense, the essay takes up one of the major themes of "Occupation: Writer": that of inventing a style which can adequately convey the contemporary reality of Quebec. Aquin also dwells in this piece on the role of the reader, a subject he will come back to in a 1974 essay, " 'The Disappearance in Language of the Poet' (Mallarmé)," in which he advocates that the reader should transfer his psychological investment in the literary work from the characters or the person of the author to the formal complexity of the work itself. In all these essays, then, any discussion of the writer and his role in society inevitably passes through the central question of style. Aquin's mentors, however, would appear to have changed: Sartrean existentialism and the theology of decolonization seem less important now than the baroque aesthetics of Joyce, Nabokov and Borges, though the two tendencies co-exist and intertwine in Aquin's second published novel, *Trou de mémoire* (*Blackout*).

In another 1974 essay—"*Joual*: Haven or Hell?"—Aquin returns to a subject touched upon in "Literature and Alienation": the use of *joual*, a Montreal working-class dialect, in literary texts. His position on the question is consistent, though at first sight somewhat surprising. One might have thought that *joual*, which Aquin defines as a form of linguistic subversion, would have been exactly the kind of *malheur d'expression* that he had been seeking since 1961, especially as other authors were using *joual* at the time in an attempt to create a national literary identity or style.[5] Aquin's reasons for rejecting *joual* as a literary language are, then, worth examining in some detail.

The most obvious problem with *joual* is that it defines itself in the first instance not against English, but against French, thus dividing the creative energy of French Canadians as they fight a war of cultural independence on two fronts instead of one. How important is it, in 1974, to strive for a national linguistic identity distinct from French? Clearly, for Aquin, such a struggle is merely a distraction from the real fight which is taking place between French and English Canada or between Quebec and the federal government. However, on the positive side, Aquin does allow that, by virtue of its spectacular contamination by English, *joual* can serve as a kind of immunization against more total assimilation. But such an advantage is more than offset by the fact that the debate surrounding the language question crystallizes collective consciousness at secondary levels, obscuring the real political issues in the fight for national liberation. This brings us back to the argument made in the earlier essays concerning the compensatory function of literature in a colonized society: for want of realities, there is an over-production of symbols. A further objection to the literary use of *joual* lies in the fact that the kind of creolization it implies constitutes for Aquin a form of pernicious anaemia which, in the long run, attacks thought itself; if the language lacks richness or precision, then the capacity to think in complex terms will be diminished. Once again, we see Aquin's insistence that lucidity not be sacrificed to emotion.

There is a great sadness about the last two essays printed here, both of which date from the last year of Aquin's life. "Why I Am Disenchanted with the Wonderful World of Roger Lemelin" takes the form of an open letter addressed to Aquin's employer at Les Éditions La Presse, former novelist Roger Lemelin. The griefs formulated in the letter speak for themselves and require no commentary. Suffice it to say that, in the aftermath of the confrontation, Aquin found himself unemployed and in a protracted state of depression. His unhappiness is apparent in the last piece—"The Text or the Surrounding Silence?"—which again is written in the form of an open letter, addressed this time to Michèle Favreau at *Mainmise*. Behind the vocabulary of mysticism (which one should not dismiss as mere rhetoric—it is a constant throughout Aquin's writing, though the dosage varies) one senses a longing for release, a desire for the silence of the margins. "Occupation: Writer" had ended with a rhetorical affirmation: "My passport has already expired. But then, I will never leave my native land again. I want to stay here. I live in my country." The letter to Favreau echoes that sentiment, but transposed in the key of mystical resignation: "There is no getting out, which is why I stay. I stay and wait for the end of an endless flight."

The letter was published in November 1976, the same month as the Parti Québécois was swept into power on a wave of nationalist sentiment which for once had a firm political basis. What Aquin had called for as early as 1962 had at last come about. Aquin would spend the rest of that month sitting by his telephone, waiting for the call from René Lévesque. The call never came and Aquin shot himself on March 15, 1977. In the note he left for his wife, he wrote: "I feel destroyed. I can't put myself back together and I don't want to. It is what I have chosen. I feel peaceful and my act is positive, the act of someone who is alive.

And don't forget that I have always known that I would be the one to choose the moment. My life has reached its end. I have lived intensely and now it's over."[6]

Notes

1. *Prochain Épisode* (Montreal: Cercle du Livre de France, 1965); translated under the same title by Penny Williams (Toronto: McClelland & Stewart, 1967). *Trou de mémoire* (Montreal: Cercle du Livre de France, 1968); translated by Alan Brown as *Blackout* (Toronto: Anansi, 1974). *L'Antiphonaire* (Montreal: Cercle du Livre de France, 1969); translated by Alan Brown as *The Antiphonary* (Toronto: Anansi, 1973). *Neige noire* (Montreal: La Presse, Collection "Écrivains des Deux Mondes," 1974); translated by Sheila Fischman as *Hamlet's Twin* (Toronto: McClelland & Stewart, 1979).
2. For an excellent bibliography of Aquin's works and secondary material, see *La Revue d'histoire littéraire du Québec et du Canada français* 7 (Winter-Spring 1984) and 10 (Summer-Autumn 1985). On Aquin as an essayist, see Anthony Purdy, "Form and (Dis-)content. The Writer, Language and Society in the Essays of Hubert Aquin," *French Review* LIX, no. 6 (May 1986), pp. 885–93, and Patricia Smart, "Hubert Aquin, essayiste," in *L'Essai et la prose d'idées au Québec*, Archives des lettres canadiennes, tome VI (Montréal: Fides, 1985), pp. 513-25.
3. The *Édition critique de l'oeuvre d'Hubert Aquin* (ÉDAQ) is the work of a nation-wide group of scholars which was formed in 1980 under the auspices of the Département d'études littéraires at the University of Quebec at Montreal. ÉDAQ's schedule allows for the publication of 21 volumes between 1988–89 and 1991–92.
4. For a discussion of Aquin's view of history in *Prochain Épisode* and the early essays, see Anthony Purdy, "De 'L'Art de la défaite' à 'Prochain Épisode': un récit unique?" *Voix et images* X, no. 3 (Spring 1985), pp. 113–25.
5. The debate surrounding the use of *joual* goes back to the publication of *Les Insolences du Frère Untel* by Jean-Paul Desbiens (Brother Pierre-Jérôme) in 1960 (Montreal: Les Éditions de l'Homme). A number of writers were using *joual* fairly systematically in their works during the nineteen-sixties and seventies, sometimes for local colour, sometimes for comic or realistic effect and sometimes as a political gesture.
6. The most complete account of Aquin's suicide and the events leading up to it are to be found in Gordon Sheppard and Andrée Yanacopoulo, *Signé Hubert Aquin. Enquête sur le suicide d'un écrivain* (Montreal: Boréal Express, 1985).

Dangerous Understanding

The journal *Liberté*[1] can be regarded as an act of aggression. What we are doing today in French Canada is closer to plotting than playing. We are opting for explosion, upheaval and attack.

The "system" in which we are caught is subtle and diffuse. The Church, the schools, the federal and provincial governments—these are its most visible structures; but it would be naive to think they are the only ones or the most stable. The fact is that the 'system' is based primarily on the unwritten and unspeakable beliefs of our collective psyche; these are the secret foundations of order that constitute the focus of our attention. We are dealing with a collective unconscious, the protean product of two centuries of repressed desire. It is high time that it saw the light of day.

One would have to be a saint or a hypocrite to deny that systematic destruction is a very pleasant little pastime. Killing sacred cows is, after all, the liveliest sport there is, and one of the healthiest. But it *is* a

1

sport. And it would be wrong of us to upset the Province of Quebec (or, if you prefer, the State of Quebec) for the sole purpose of providing it with a display of intellectual terrorism.

We want to understand. Just because Quebec has embarked on an irresistible programme of social change does not mean that thought has to be put off until tomorrow. On the contrary, the current turmoil makes the very act of thinking more indispensable than ever, while at the same time creating more problems for it to solve and secretly undermining it. Five or even three years ago, one could point the finger at censorship and even use it as a scapegoat. Today it wears a mask and uses methods that are all the more effective for their subtlety. Today's censorship goes undenounced. We want to denounce it. We want to understand the reality in which we are immersed and which carries us along on its tide of events and misconceptions.

We at *Liberté* have another vice. We value language—lyrical or discursive, magical or sober—and all that so-called men of action look down on under the name of literature and poetry. Language is a form of life and, in its own wonderful way, a mode of action. At any rate, it is no more futile to write than to act, especially as what we call action stems from an order created by thought.

Is *Liberté* a politically committed journal? I can only say that, given our invocation of the word *freedom*, it would be improper for me to speak on behalf of my colleagues, who have given me no mandate to act as their spokesman. I can, however, if pressed, go so far as to say that Lafcadio is not our super-ego and that the publication of a monthly journal is the antithesis of a gratuitous act.[2] Our very title, which also translates an idea, warns us not to confuse commitment with mobilization. In the past three years, we have had generous friends but no silent partners. We are committed to French Canada, both by our concern and by our desire to understand and express the reality of our country. Nothing that is French Canadian is foreign to us. Our commitment is a general one, but it does not preclude the possibility of saying no on specific counts or, if necessary, on all counts.[3]

From now on, *Liberté* will appear once a month. This new rhythm will give greater intensity to our enterprise and allow us to reach a larger number of readers who, like us, are interested in defining French Canada as it evolves and in understanding the determining influences and forces of attraction at play outside its borders. The youth of those who are associated with *Liberté* is not a function of their average age. It lies, to my mind, in their energy, their openness and their ability to grow. We have no positions to defend but many we plan to attack or, at least, to examine very closely. Youth, regardless of the age of those who are blessed with it, does not defend. It attacks.

["Comprendre dangereusement."
Liberté III, no. 5 (November 1961): 679–80.]

Editor's Notes

1. *Liberté* was founded in 1959. Aquin was the journal's editor from November 1961 to July 1962.
2. The character Lafcadio appears in André Gide's *Les Caves du Vatican* (1914; variously translated as *The Vatican Cellars*, *The Vatican Swindle* and *Lafcadio's Adventures*). He embodies the idea of the gratuitous act ("l'acte gratuit") which, in his pursuit of personal freedom, he takes to the absurd extreme of murder.
3. The French contains an allusion to Paul-Émile Borduas' 1948 modernist manifesto *Refus global*.

Form and (Dis-)content

Happiness is a question of ethics. I find it hard to dissociate these two terms which so many religious thinkers have seen as linked, but which many "progressive" minds persist in treating as separate entities.

Happiness is possible only within a system one accepts and, ultimately, is really nothing more than that acceptance. Of course, acceptance can take many forms, from serenity to Christian resignation, from a sunny disposition to an Isaac complex. But this wide variety of attitudes, some of them mutually exclusive, conceals a common outlook—one of acceptance, to my mind the least revolutionary attitude possible.

People who are happy are counter-revolutionaries! They can be made to swallow anything and still make the best of it, just as good Christians are able to rejoice in their misfortunes by turning them into trials. Once the process of acceptance has started, what is there to stop it? Besides, people who really want happiness find it, because the fact is that happiness is a matter of will.

Look at the great characters of fiction. Is it not significant that they engage in the pursuit of happiness until it is theirs for the taking and then decide they do not want it? If Mathilde de La Mole and Madame de Mortsauf[1] are inaccessible and untouchable, it is because the men who talk of killing themselves on their account nurture an unconscious desire for them to remain that way. And the woman met *Last Year in Marienbad*—the important thing is *not* to have met her. Resnais' entire film is based on that obscure, faltering desire to refuse a source of happiness, even past happiness. The convergence of so many missed opportunities in the universal folklore of fiction poses a problem for happy people. Why do happy people (and they do exist!) feed on these sublime disasters and glorious failures? For reasons of catharsis, Aristotle would say; but perhaps, too, so they can feel a little grander than they are.

For those who have chosen happiness have chosen not to be heroes. I would even say, at the risk of seeming paradoxical, that anyone who chooses happiness gives up, or ought to give up, the possibility of being an artist.

What can artists possibly teach me if they take it into their heads to be happy? How can they go on surprising me? I have no need of works born in the debilitating climate of acceptance. Whether they be novelists, poets or painters, artists are professionals of unhappiness. And I mean professionals, not amateurs!

My point is this: the greatness of a work of art is not necessarily proportional to its creator's unhappiness. That would really be too easy. Unhappiness, too, is an art. The unhappiness I am talking about, the only kind that is productive, is the sign of a deep commitment; it is a vocation and not just a matter of chance. Far from considering the artist as a victim who uses art to compensate for his lot in life, I see him as a hero who takes full responsibility for the destiny he has chosen.

As I see it, unhappiness involves a higher level of consciousness, making it the royal road of the artist who wants to express reality, to recreate it, to give it new life and a new form. Seen in this light, unhappiness becomes a privileged way of experiencing life and a preparation for artistic endeavour.

My admiration for Baudelaire, Dostoevsky, Balzac, Pascal, Pirandello or Proust, who lived their "difficulty of being" to the full, producing great works in the process, is matched only by the pity I feel for the lesser unfortunates with their tragic air, the masochists of small output, born to choke on the crust that is theirs. They are amateurs; what more can I say?

And here I can't help taking a dig at our own artists who, with a few exceptions both living and dead, exist in a psychological and social cocoon. The sad truth is that too many of our artists are happy and in fact accept the very society they criticize so vociferously. They are devoured by the system and, when they do produce, draw only on the most superficial aspect of their being—their talent. I won't try to hide the fact that, for me, so much "artistic" happiness is cause for great concern.

Yet, if I look at myself dispassionately, I do not see myself as some kind of vulture, attracted by the misfortune of others. What interests me is works of art—the great ones, the ones I regret not having created myself, the ones I would have given ten years of my life for. When I find myself face to face with a great work of art, I have the unbearable feeling that I have been robbed (which shows, I know, that I still haven't chosen my "vocation"). It is not a feeling (and it causes me great distress to say so) that I have often had before the works of our native soil. The bulk of our novels, for instance, are direly moralistic. And God knows there is nothing farther from beauty and tragedy than morality. Morality is the death of tragedy. Nietzsche taught us that. Canadian literature has many dramas of conscience, but no tragedies. In short, every morality is a morality of happiness.

An old proverb—probably of English origin—has it that the French Canadian is passive and, as one of my teachers liked to say, somewhat sheeplike. In other words—my own—French Canadians seem happy. We have known this for a long time, even when it comes to politics. The political leaders we have chosen to lionize have been the most accepting. We have been taught to admire Lafontaine, G.-E. Cartier, Laurier, Bourassa, but Papineau gets short shrift in the way of respect.[2] We are politically happy because we have agreed to trade in flags and bilingual cheques, but never in the essentials. Two centuries of conquest have turned us into happy and grateful counter-revolutionaries.

In the revolutionary order there is no room for moderates, just as amateurs have no place in art. There is an obvious connection between these two aspects of our national life; my intuition tells me so, and for the moment that will have to suffice. . . .

From our low productivity, both in art and in politics, I do not conclude that we are a happy people. At least, I do not accept that happiness. In assuming my identity as a French Canadian, I am choosing unhappiness. And I believe that, as a conquered minority, we are profoundly unhappy. We have been taught to reduce our unhappiness—both collective and individual—to its weakest expression, to accept it, to make the best of it. We have been taught to laugh about it, just as a cripple is told to smile.

But there will no doubt appear, in French Canada, politicians who are capable of a lucid appraisal of this "unhappiness" and who will take it to its logical end. May there also be writers and artists capable of giving form to their discontent.

["Le bonheur d'expression."
Liberté III, no. 6 (December 1961): 741–43.]

Editor's Notes

1. Mathilde de La Mole and Madame de Mortsauf are characters in, respectively, Stendhal's *The Red and the Black* and Balzac's *The Lily of the Valley*.
2. Louis-Joseph Papineau (1786–1871) was regarded as the leader of the *Patriotes* prior to the 1837–1838 rebellion, in which, however, he took no active part; he lived in exile from 1837 until 1844, when amnesty was granted to the rebels. Louis-Hippolyte Lafontaine (1807–1864) and Georges-Étienne Cartier (1814–1873) were both supporters of Papineau—though Lafontaine opposed the call to arms in 1837—before holding high political office from the late 1840s through, in Cartier's case, the 1860s. Wilfrid Laurier (1841–1919) was prime minister of Canada from 1896 to 1911. Henri Bourassa (1868–1952) was a nationalist politician, journalist and pamphleteer; in 1910 he founded the daily newspaper *Le Devoir*.

The Politics of Existence

One of the lessons we have learned from the RIN Congress[1] is that, for some of the people we respect, nationalism in all its forms is like the kiss of death. This prejudice (and prejudice it is in the context of today's separatism which "advocates" independence) feeds as much on the ghost of Duplessis[2] and the more or less bitter memory of the nineteen-thirties brand of patriotism as on the old political failures which define our history. Why, in the name of a past which is held to be determining, would we refuse a future which we still have the power to shape, at least according to the philosophies of Aquinas and Sartre? This opposition to the idea of Quebec's independence is paradoxically quite typical of the French Canadian—conquered in every fibre of his being, let down time and again by his leaders to the point of being traumatized by so many setbacks.

For some people, separatism brings to mind this history of disenchantment and kindles the fear that another, even more disappointing chapter will be added to it. Which is why separatist leaders have no easy task when they try to convince their fellow-countrymen, who have so often been had, to take yet another chance. They are not suggesting that we dig in our heels, or make demands or defend what already is, but that we rebuild from scratch a country we have grown used to regarding as not altogether ours. They are not advocating an improvement in the terms of an old compromise, but a total national revolution. But did we not long ago give up all idea of revolution, with the possible exception of a local one which would not jeopardize our security within Confederation? After all, our status as political dependents does bring with it a certain security. The words are hardly out of my mouth than I am revolted by the hypocrisy of it all. We are the victims of an equivocation: the fact that we are not at war gives us the illusion of peace and security. As French Canadians, we have reached a point in the struggle against English Canada where, weary and exhausted, we are tempted to throw in the towel. We are the weaker of the two, both economically and politically; we shall go on growing weaker and weaker, and a certain persistence in decline seems more reassuring than any resumption of hostilities. We are beaten before we have started. Confederation has institutionalized this inequality and, even if we go along with the system, we shall wear ourselves out in defence of our status as a conquered people. If we remain in Confederation, our history is written in advance and allows no possibility of starting afresh. We will be the junior partner, weak and, moreover, weary, and none of the possible variants of our condition, from more or less autonomous to more or less centralized, will change the present balance in this unfair fight.

Since I have spoken of war, I might as well make a clean breast of it. I know that hostility toward English Canadians is not a respectable sentiment, even in separatist circles. Unfortunately, I am a woefully emotional separatist who finds it healthier to acknowledge his negative feelings toward English Canadians, if only to preclude the possibility of their finding expression in some act of collective violence.

The fact is, I attach a certain value to the ill feelings I harbour against English Canadians, since these feelings are at the very root of my separatist convictions. French Canada's minority status is defined historically in relation to English Canada's aggressively held position as a majority. This unwanted but constant confrontation has conditioned the French Canadian to a whole range of habits and attitudes which he has yet to grow out of and which he can really leave behind only by becoming independent. And even then, who knows? In certain cases, xenophobia is known to persist long after the last foreigner has left the country. The after-effects of our hostility toward English Canadians are still with us. Separatism—the desire to separate, to become independent—can arise only within a relationship between two individuals, two groups, two peoples. Independence cannot be achieved instantaneously, by divine right, at no cost; it is something which is won from someone else who, rightly or wrongly, is seen to be standing in the way. For all these reasons, I think the word *separatism* appropriately describes the various independence movements in existence in Quebec today. We want to separate. *A priori*, separation is neither good nor bad. Only a confused or an anglicized mind would assert that separation is synonymous with isolation. Without English Canadians, or without the annoyance that every one of us has felt toward them, we would not today be pondering the problem of independence. From a historical point of view, this emotional opposition is fundamental, and it would be bordering on Jansenism to try to deny it. Ill feelings, deep annoyance and a sense of emotional humiliation are at the source of all separatism. We must not seek to disguise our national sin; nor must we yield, impulsively or otherwise, to the negative feelings to which it can give rise.

If we own up to our ill feelings, we will have a better chance not only of understanding ourselves but also of accepting ourselves in all honesty. It will also help us to understand the impatience that English Canadians feel in return at having us on their hands, if not on their backs! On this score, they are no less dishonest than we are.

But despite the important and productive role that anti-English feeling and its offshoots have played historically, they have, to my mind, no importance in political terms. In other words, while our minority separatism has evolved against *English* Canadians, when it comes to actually achieving independence it will be against *French* Canadians that we shall have to fight. It is on the political stage, and nowhere else, that something positive can come of a history which has its origins —both individual and collective—in an emotional refusal to accept minority status.

Now that I have shown my ill feelings (with which, to paraphrase André Gide, one makes good politics), I can move on to the many questions that the separatist issue raises for me. The separatist movement, taken as a whole, would appear to be a national phenomenon, but I doubt that it is yet a political one. However, it would not take much for it to become political, and it is precisely this very fine line which is to be crossed (and which, I might as well say it now, I hope *will* be crossed) that interests me.

One thing that has struck me for some time now is the growing number of separatists I run into. The conversions are coming thick enough and fast enough to go to the heads of our new messiahs. Yet Mr. Chaput has performed no miracles; he has not turned water into wine. The most he has done is to resign from his job as a federal civil servant.[3] Nor has Raymond Barbeau[4] performed any miracles; nor has Raoul Roy.[5] And yet I have the distinct impression that we are faced with a quasi-religious phenomenon. In fact, it would not be the first time in French Canada that politics had been taken for religion.

What causes me most concern is that there may be no correlation between the large number of conversions to separatism and any real progress towards Quebec's independence. The reason I think this is that, in a sense, once one is converted to separatism one can stop worrying about it, just as in certain Christian denominations faith renders works superfluous. As for separatist faith, is there a single French Canadian who has not at some time, if only in a moment of abandon or lucidity, been touched by it? Who among us would dare say that separatism in itself is bad? Oh, I know only too well that there are those who do say it, but the logical answer for them, if they were consistent, would be systematic assimilation to the English.

Faith, then, we more or less have, but when it comes to works, our separatists seem to me to be more contemplative than charitable or, if you prefer, more mystical than effective. Our separatism is a kind of enchantment or possession; but the morning after, when the spell has worn off, the French Canadian goes back to an unchanged reality—still federal and still bilingual.

Our separatists deliver a great many sermons on the mount and not enough political speeches.

For example, a separatist spoke recently of the possibility of taking our case to the United Nations, with the idea that we might have our independence granted by that body. Which only goes to show just how far out of touch some people are with political reality. Apart from the pleasant trip to New York that it would entail, the plan bears all the indications of an impossible dream, blind both to the nature of the international organization and to the historical precedents, which are such as to discourage any attempt of the kind.

To my mind, this kind of thinking underestimates the real level of political education of French Canadians, which is high. French Canadians will not go off on a wild goose chase, or at least have no desire to do so. If it comes to a choice between a losing political situation and a pipe dream, they would rather stick with. . . Confederation.

And God knows Confederation is no paradise. Even if it is not exactly political hell, it is a kind of constitutional purgatory or, if you prefer, a rich man's funeral for a poor minority. Its one advantage is that it exists, or pre-exists if that makes sense, and has of course reminded French Canadians of their numerical and political strength and of their ambitions. Without wishing to appear paradoxical, I would say that Confederation deserves a vote of thanks for having given birth, in spite of itself, to the separatist movements.

The greatest enemies of independence are not to be found in Ottawa but in Quebec City. As yet, nothing has forced the Lesage government to declare itself anti-separatist (one might even think at times that its wide-ranging autonomism is paving the way for independence), but there is no doubt that if Marcel Chaput were to run in the elections against Jean Lesage, Lesage would have to define himself politically as a defender of Confederation.[6] Shall I tell you what I really think about all this? Daniel Johnson is in a position to corner Jean Lesage on this question; if he were tempted to exploit the independence issue, he could easily become the catalyst for an anti-separatist liberal government and, given the polarization of positions within any parliament, he himself would in turn come forward as a leader for independence. But let us hope that I am imagining the worst.[7]

It is not terribly difficult to trigger French Canadians' nationalism, something which has been done periodically in the name of conflicting ideologies ever since the tribunes of the people discovered that a member of a minority group feels as if he had been skinned alive. The only time that French Canadians actually did anything about their situation was in 1837. Since then they have taken refuge behind stirring nationalist speeches and bilingual cheques.

And that is just what I am afraid of now: that the nationalist fervour will yet again use itself up in words and emotions without ever giving rise to the only form of political action that I recognize as sound—the electoral fight and parliamentary process. If this transition does not occur soon, if the ideological tenets of separatism do not assume the concrete form of electoral ambition, thus forcing the enemies of independence to show their hand, then the current surge of feeling could well end up drowning in the tide of its own glorious but ineffectual lyricism.

I am not an advocate of the *coup d'état*, of the *putsch* or of its related forms; even if, in retrospect, yesterday's *coup d'état* seems to me to have been inevitable, I think tomorrow's should still be denounced. There is no getting away from the fact that we are in North America and that we invented neither the tango nor the politics of revolutionary dominoes. We live in a political context coloured by British parliamentarianism and we like things to run smoothly. Violence cannot be learned overnight; politics, fortunately, can. That is our only chance. Let us not grow careless just when we are starting to have some kind of method.

I am hoping, then, for a rapid political crystallization of all our separatist ideologies. Only such a crystallization will give the French-Canadian people an idea of the conflicting political forces at play.

Independence cannot be proposed in a vacuum; it has to have a name, a political framework, a platform and, of course, good candidates. If the separatist leaders fight shy of taking a stand on the major political issues that divide French Canada, they will never get to first base in politics. One cannot enter politics without being either to the left or the right, without opting for one position rather than another. In politics, you cannot sit back and rely on defensive strategy; you have to attack and take risks. It would be annoying to see the New Party[8] proclaimed as the left (and the only viable left) when separatist ideology can just as well take a socialist form. It is unfortunate that, until now, separatism has automatically been identified with the right. There is nothing to prevent independence from being achieved within a socialist framework. Once the revolutionary path is taken, one cannot stop halfway; the revolution in Quebec, and I quote Marcel Rioux, will be total or will be no revolution at all.[9]

Independence is an intellectual concept. We need to know in what political and parliamentary guise this creature of reason will emerge. We also need to know who will be responsible for realizing this dream, who will lead us to the Promised Land and by what road. As a citizen— and it is time for me to state my prejudices—I am a separatist, but I am dissatisfied with the way in which this old revolutionary dream of every French Canadian is being interpreted.

The outbreaks of nationalism which have shaken our minority in the past have ended more or less in failure, no doubt because our nationalists wanted, not to put an end to a union predicated on our own dependence, but to improve the terms of that dependence. Even today there are sincere nationalists who ask Ottawa to grant them their rights, never gauging the extent to which this type of nationalism tends to perpetuate a bond of dependence between a querulous minority and a more or less conciliatory majority. The fact is that those who accept Confederation accept their minority status; they accept a condition which consists, first and foremost, precisely in the making of demands. Our entire history is characterized by this same confusion of nationalism with the defence of our rights—two positions which, to my mind, are diametrically opposed. The defender of our rights is already resigned to our minority status, whereas the nationalist, who puts the nation first, wants its wardship to end. True nationalists want separation and independence, not the perpetuation of provincial or minority status.

It would be useful, in the interests not of isolating some of our number but of understanding one another, to divide French Canadian citizens and those in public life into two political camps, according to whether or not they want an independent French Canada. We would then have two categories of French-Canadian nationalists: those who oppose Confederation and those who defend it. A middle ground is often invoked, involving the reconstitution of Confederation as a pact between two equal nations. But I find it hard to imagine that such a plan, which might have worked a hundred years ago, could be carried out today. It would be difficult for the French Canadian to feel equal in an unchanged situation in which he has always been the junior partner; besides, what kind of system would give political equality to a demographic minority? So, I discount these utopian possibilities to which certain federalists, whose intentions are good but whose eyesight is failing, still cling.

To come back to my previous distinction: in one camp we have the federalists with their demands, in the other the separatists. These two groups constitute the two poles of thought currently dividing French Canada, and if the Parliament of Quebec is to reflect these two deeply rooted tendencies of French-Canadian thought and not two variants of one and the same attachment to a confederative system, then I think we need to insist on this double polarization. Jean Lesage and Daniel

Johnson are the leaders of two *provincial* parties with essentially the same party line: that the Province of Quebec must have its rightful place in Confederation. But let a separatist party sit in the Quebec legislature, even in the opposition benches, and then the Quebec Parliament will, I think, reflect the true tendencies of the French-Canadian nation, express its real conflicts and perhaps succeed in resolving them. But once again, for that to happen, separatism has to be seen as a political force and not simply as a cult. The conversion of French Canadians to independence is a first step; but we must not wait for that conversion to be unanimous for it to be effective; it will never be unanimous, any more than support for Confederation has been unanimous.

No doubt the public has been convinced by the rhetorical precautions taken hitherto by separatists in order to prove they are harmless; but the separatists themselves appear now to be conforming to the reassuring image they have created for the benefit of others. Peacefulness is a virtue when compared with the prospect of violence associated with any revolutionary movement; but to be too peaceful and too patient is to run the risk of exasperating those elements of the population in Quebec that are receptive to real change. These days, separatism is played *moderato cantabile;* it is a sign of the times or one more manifestation of our sense of democracy. But we cannot afford to dream. The public expects something more radical, more open, more revolutionary. At least, I do. I do not expect revolutionaries with machine guns and uniforms, but I do expect revolutionaries who are no more afraid of words than of realities. By saying nothing we run the risk of being too clever by half; we have stopped talking about socialism (in this respect, the New Party takes some beating, as it too avoids the subject); we have no position on the question of education, of church or public schools; we line up neither to the right nor to the left of the present government, wanting rather to be seen as being *above* it.

I have a feeling that our separatist leaders model themselves more on English-Canadian archetypes than on French-Canadian ones. We have been misled by English Canadians into accepting a certain type of leader, more of a negotiator than a revolutionary; Mackenzie King is an example and Louis Saint-Laurent his French-Canadian counterpart. Such emulation is unfortunate in that our political leaders have assumed the superficial aspects of their English-Canadian models without adopting any of their real dynamism, their initiative or their inventiveness. The revolutionary tradition in French Canada has been subject to a vast and constant programme of repression, of which our political leaders are the product.

To embark on a revolution is to make a complete break with the history of mistakes and compromises on which the political structure of Quebec is founded. Politically, independence is diametrically opposed to autonomy, even if, from a historical point of view, it can be considered as its extension. The separatist and the autonomist have nothing in common; one wants Quebec to secede, the other wants it to participate, as a more or less integral part, in Confederation.

Confusion arises perhaps from the fact that both separatists and autonomists are in conflict with Ottawa; but such confusion should soon be dispelled. The separatists, logically, must consider the government of Quebec as their sole enemy. And if the provincial government, no matter how autonomist, is the enemy, then it must also be the target of the strategies we deploy; it is this government which must be overthrown, unless we are content to convert it.

If the strategy I am advocating here seems precipitate, it is because I believe that history itself will not wait. What we are seeing today is that the separatists have made enemies in Ottawa, while the Lesage government continues to rule with the tacit or turbid blessing of the revolutionaries. In war, as in politics, it is not good strategy to drag one's feet. On the contrary, to be effective a policy must be quick and flexible —at the very least quicker than that of the opposition. If we wait for the government of Quebec, with the opposition hot on its heels on this issue, to establish a decent autonomy in the province, it will be all the more difficult to persuade the voters to accept a national revolution. Without knowing it, the Liberals are perhaps laying the groundwork for independence; but they are doing it so well that they are able to sabotage any possibility of independence really being achieved. Independence cannot be seen as just another piece of legislation, to be voted on as though nothing were at stake. It is a revolutionary political concept and must be presented to French Canadians as such. To disguise or play down the revolutionary significance of independence would be to underestimate our countrymen; and then, such legalistic attempts to make independence palatable, carried out with an overly self-conscious cleverness, will prevent the real opposing forces at play from coming to the fore and defining themselves. The separatist speeches I read written up in the newspapers tend to downplay the problems of independence and to sugar the pill for an electorate which ought really to be confronted as soon as possible with a power struggle it will eventually have to decide at the polls.

I am in favour of Quebec's independence, and I want to go on being so; but I want someone to offer me a political choice, an option, a decision. . . . I wish that someone would propose a national revolution as such—and not as a chapter appended to the Imperial Statutes or as a diplomatic treaty to be ruled on at the United Nations. Yes, I want independence. But I could never be satisfied with an *essence* of independence; I would like it also to *exist*, to take a specific form and have a well-defined political programme. Independence is not necessarily an improvement on our present condition within Confederation; independence will not and cannot be idyllic. It can only be a revolution and, as such, it represents a political step which is important but fraught with difficulty, a step which a people remains free to want to take or not.

["L'existence politique." *Liberté* IV, no. 21 (March 1962): 67–76.][10]

Editor's Notes

1. The RIN (Rassemblement pour l'Indépendance Nationale) was founded in 1960 by Marcel Chaput and André D'Allemagne. It would become a political party in March 1963, taking nine percent of the vote in the 1966 provincial elections. On its dissolution in October 1968, most of its members would follow their leader Pierre Bourgault and join with René Lévesque's Mouvement Souveraineté-Association (MSA) to form the Parti Québécois. For a short time in the spring of 1964, Aquin would be first vice-president of the RIN for the Montreal region.
2. Maurice Duplessis, leader of the Union Nationale and premier of Quebec (1936–1939 and 1944–1959), had died in September 1959, opening the door for Jean Lesage's Quiet Revolution.
3. Marcel Chaput, co-founder of the RIN and author of *Pourquoi je suis séparatiste* (1961), had resigned in 1961 from his position as a Defence Research Council scientist in Ottawa after being suspended for attending a conference at which he had openly endorsed independence. In December 1962 he would leave the RIN and announce the formation of the Parti Républicain du Québec (PRQ).
4. Author of *J'ai choisi l'indépendance* (1961), Raymond Barbeau had founded in 1957 the right-wing independence movement, the Alliance Laurentienne, which would be dissolved in 1963 in favour of the PRQ.
5. Raoul Roy was the founder, in September 1960, of the Action Socialiste pour l'Indépendance du Québec. In 1959 he had founded *La Revue socialiste*.
6. Jean Lesage was elected Liberal premier of Quebec in June 1960. Re-elected in No-

vember 1962 using the slogan "Maîtres chez nous" ("Masters in our own house"), he would lose the 1966 election to Daniel Johnson's Union Nationale.

7. Elected leader of the Union Nationale in 1961, Daniel Johnson would win the provincial elections of June 1966 and would die in office in September 1968. His book *Égalité ou indépendance* would be published in 1965.

8. By the end of 1961, two distinct factions had emerged within the Quebec wing of the New Party (NDP), the French-speaking nationalists demanding a separate party for Quebec and the English-speaking federalists preferring closer ties with the federal party. The nationalists would make their move in 1962–63, forming the Parti Socialiste du Québec (PSQ) to contest provincial elections. The party would fold within a year, to be replaced in 1965 by a provincial NDP.

9. Aquin is paraphrasing a statement made by Marcel Rioux in a round table discussion published in *Liberté* IV, no. 19–20 (January-February 1962), pp. 24–53.

10. The same issue of *Liberté* contains interviews with Marcel Chaput (pp. 145–49) and Raymond Barbeau (pp. 150–58).

The Cultural Fatigue of French Canada

A total earth requires nations that are fully aware.

Teilhard de Chardin[1]

The minds of French-Canadian "thinkers" are infused with unconscious relativism. Except for a prudent minority who manage to maintain an independent or neutral stance, any intellectual who attempts to understand the French-Canadian problem is subjected to mental vivisection by those who try to determine which side of the fence he is really on. And as soon as his brain has been surgically classified, his ability to know anything is immediately challenged and it is assumed that his particular conditioning is known once and for all. Our scholars have encouraged this sort of relativism themselves, and it inevitably turns against them; thus it becomes useless to give any credence at all to a writer like Michel Brunet, a historian of the "nationalist" school or, from a different angle, Jean-Charles Falardeau, a sociologist of the so-called "Father Lévesque" school and an avowed federalist. Labels, although they are not always quite so blatant or undeserved, are exclusive things, and I know very few journalists or academics who have not in this way come to be identified with a specific, closed, ideological group. Ideas tend to be automatically considered as being strongly representative, and as a result they become connected with a particular bias or school of thought and lose their dialectical effectiveness. By considering their rivals simply as products of a narrow conditioning, intellectuals in French Canada have come to resemble deaf people shouting at one another; at the same time they have destroyed any hope one might have had in their own powers of intellection.

For my part, I refuse to accept the idea that any one person can dogmatically speak of reality as though his special way of presenting it were completely objective; on the other hand, I do not want to get involved in ideological skirmishes and start accusing others of presenting only a partial view of a reality they are trying to make me understand in its entirety. That tactic is too easy. Besides, I hold that the act of thinking has a definite power of elucidation that no conditioning can account for. In other words, the real dialectic is in dialogue, and not in two parallel monologues. It is still possible to think, and it is such an important act that even if it is done by a social or political "adversary," it should not be thought of as a hymn that only members of one's own congregation can sing. An adversary may discover just as much truth and may understand just as much about reality as the person on "my" side or one who shares "my" views.

Situations of this sort must be defined from within the dialectical tension between different viewpoints and situations—not from the outside, or from above. The dialectical process generates lucidity and logic but under no circumstances should it ever stoop to the level of opposition between two political parties which, as we know, by their very nature refuse any attempt at comprehension. Political partisanship is a means of action, not a mode of thinking: at best, parties think of themselves as "ideological," locked into a preconceived system of society whose perfect self-image should reveal how precarious or idealistic it is.

If I make these precautionary remarks, it is because I want to stress clearly that the study I am undertaking, based on an article by Pierre Elliott Trudeau called "New Treason of the Intellectuals,"[2] is not completely gratuitous; nor is it an underhanded attempt to prove that Trudeau's ideas are only the relatively brilliant reflection of a different option from one used to define me! His article is clearly an attempt at rational argumentation, and I would hate to see it construed to be simply the "conditioned reflex" of a political activist or an anti-separatist.

Nationalism and War

Pierre Elliott Trudeau's opinions and thoughts first struck me as forming a fairly coherent logical structure, nicely articulated in a vigorous style. And since he himself adopted a rational approach to his subject, I shall try to debate with him on the same level.

I agree with him that nationalism has often been a detestable, even unspeakable thing: the crimes committed in its name are perhaps even worse than the atrocities perpetrated in the name of liberty. In the nineteenth century, the resurgence of nationalistic feeling was marked by wars which gravely tarnished every possible form of nationalism and any system of thought stemming from it:

> the nation-state idea has caused wars to become more and more total over the last two centuries; and that is the idea I take issue with so vehemently. . . . And there will be no end to wars between nations until . . . the nation ceases to be the basis of the state. As for interstate wars, they will end only if the states give up that obsession whose very essence makes them exclusive and intolerant: sovereignty.[3]

The connection made between war and nationalism ("the nation-state idea") seems somewhat problematic.[4] The convergence of these two phenomena, even several times in succession, does not in itself establish a real causal relationship. The resurgence of wars poses a philosophical problem that is too easily restricted to its coincidence with nationalistic movements or outbursts of religious or ideological "statism."

War is a collective—or world-wide—extension of the notion of conflict, and I tend to believe that if war were studied scientifically (which strikes me as being as urgently necessary as the desire for peace), perhaps we would begin to discover basic explanations related to the entire human phenomenon. Until now, thinkers have either opposed war or else devised plans for peace, like those of Abbé de Saint-Pierre in 1713 and Jeremy Bentham in 1789; curiously, however, few have used their minds to study the phenomenon of war. A kind of social or individual repression causes men of learning to bury their heads where war is concerned. It took many centuries and one lucid man to separate the earth from the cosmos, and several centuries more before a certain Viennese doctor made the subconscious and its sexual fountainhead a subject for study; in the same way, war has produced a variety of convictions, emotions and mental blocks in men of learning, but it has never generated much lucidity. Such reactions are so prevalent that war, one of the most destructive phenomena in the history of man,[5] finds itself subjected, so to speak, to all sorts of hasty and partial explanations: wars are caused by God, Jews, economic conflicts, assassinations of princes, royal families, munitions manufacturers, nationalism, and so on, depending on the ideology of whoever is using war as an argument. Thus, in Trudeau's article, war is seen as resulting from nationalism, although the author never makes clear what correlation there is between this micro-phenomenon (the emergence of the nation-state) and its gigantic corollary which has steeped humanity in blood from the beginning. If reflection is to go beyond mere appearance in its search for a profound and comprehensive system of explanations for undeniable though perhaps still circumstantial coincidences, it had better not depend on dubious causality. The causal connection between wars and nationalism is fragile, and it minimizes the importance of the phenomenon of war. How can these minor historical crises be the cause of such a terrible and mysterious phenomenon, particularly since war was part of man's experience long before the emergence of nations, and since by its own extension it has also overtaken the modern super-nations?[6]

The condemnation of war, however well justified, can never be a substitute for its rational comprehension by the human mind; the same was true of sex for a long time. . . . War is a destructive and dangerous occurrence that has often been denounced; responses to it, however, have always taken the form of combat attitudes (rejection, pacifism, condemnation) rather than scientific attitudes. Total war poses a philosophical problem for mankind; preoccupied in the past by a "totality" that was never questioned, man must now study war in the same way he attempts to understand death; and, for the same reason, he must stop viewing war as a pure and undifferentiated evil. Instead of being a subject for scandal and peace conferences, war must become a field of humanistic study; it should no longer be used for instant arguments whose inherent maliciousness, too often unchallenged, acts like a bludgeon upon thought.

The "Subconscious" of Peace

War is a philosophical mystery which should be elucidated. Intimately connected with the particularity of man, war is one of his characteristic functions, and this fact should, in the minds of our thinkers, help rehabilitate what is considered to be an especially "shameful" function. If war is considered as a function, it becomes instantly associated with all the contradictory, ambivalent characteristics of other human functions. In any case, it would be difficult to consider peace without recognizing the importance of its shady "subconscious."

Who knows whether our future historians may not include in the notion of war such things as conferences on disarmament, like the ones in Geneva, for example? Such conferences are obviously an expression of conflicts whose goal is the end of all armed conflict. They are, so to speak, variants of war, and when put together with all the other variants in which history abounds, they may help us understand war as a general phenomenon resulting from communication between any two groups of whatever size. If such were the case, Geneva diplomacy and verbal clashes at the UN would come to be considered as much a part of the full definition of war as military battles; thus war would have to be considered no longer solely as a catastrophe but as a confrontation in which the less heated issues might form the basis for dialogue.[7] In so-called "primitive" societies, where great emphasis was put on unanimity, dissension was exorcized through a prescribed ritual of confrontation and combat. ("In other words, there must be no minority," wrote Claude Lévi-Strauss, and I hope no one will accuse me here of stealing his ideas!)

On the whole, these societies are egalitarian, mechanical in type, and governed by the law of unanimity. . . . The civilized peoples, on the other hand, produce a great deal of order. . . but they also produce a great deal of entropy. . . in the form of social conflicts and political struggles, which, as we saw, are the things that primitive peoples guard against . . . . The great problem of civilization has, therefore, been to maintain differentials. [They work on the basis of a difference in potential, which finds concrete expression in different forms of social hierarchy.] We have seen these ensured by means of slavery, then serfdom, and lastly with the creation of a proletariat. But as the working-class struggle tends, to some extent, to iron out the differences, our society has had to look for fresh ways of establishing differentials—colonialism and the so-called imperialist policies, for instance—that is, it has had constantly to try, either within the society itself or by subjecting conquered peoples, to create a differential between a ruling section and a section that is ruled; but such a differential is always provisional. . . . [8]

According to this view, the individual "differentials" that are quickly eliminated through ritual in primitive societies are reduced in great modern societies by collective struggles and, to an increasing extent, at the price of human lives. These differentials among classes, states, groups of states, or cultures contain the seeds of all future struggles, whatever form these struggles may take, whether military, parliamentary, or ideological. "Differentials" breed struggle; by their constant, formless, protean metamorphoses, they also form a dialectic by continually recreating two differentiated poles which will logically tend to move towards a balance between the two. This basic inequality of all civilizations can be eliminated only by relegating the inequality to a third consideration: nature. All in all, power would no longer be based on the lesser power of another group, but should be shared with it on the basis of power over inertia. This means that the problem of disarmament cannot be formulated without a total revolution of all societies; once they have purged their tension against the superior term of opposition and gone beyond it, thus being somewhat equalized in every sense, they could begin to identify themselves in relation to a new dialectic term: nature, or the cosmos. States or groups so conceived cannot be disarmed so long as there are other groups which, through differentials, force them to define themselves as *opposites*. In order to change these groups' inclination towards contradiction and struggle, it is first necessary to eliminate the original differentials between the groups.

It is misguided to expect groups divided into unequal, inferior, or differentiated divisions to bypass a stage in the dialectical process that regulates even international gatherings. There is no possible short cut for moving from a position of inferiority, of which the collectivity is painfully aware, to a position of co-operation among equals, unless perhaps this short cut simply involves the complete suppression of the minority group in question. "At the same time as we are invited to build a universal civilization, we are asked to renounce our own culture..." said Léopold Senghor, reminding us that the "universal" can exist only through the free and active participation of all the particular elements which have chosen to create it. If these particularities are really extravagant or merely strange whims, they will not long withstand the "excommunications" directed against them.

> If we had the example of a country which had unilaterally renounced its national culture and its past in order to become more progressive, more universal, then we could follow its example. But this has not happened yet. ... We are concerned to fashion a national culture which will quite simply be a protective rampart for us until the security of our whole planet can be realized.[9]

Nationalism Versus Internationalism

War, you may say, is leading us away from the main point. Not at all. If I first examined the second section of Pierre Elliott Trudeau's article, in which he establishes a causal relationship between nationalism and war, it is because this first dialectical weakness struck me, paradoxically, as the most difficult one to expose. In point of fact, the argument that nationalism causes war is very persuasive and, precisely because of the historical "evidence," it is very difficult to challenge. It is an argument which shuts people up and which, apparently based on facts (which, of course, are not open to question), is slow to reveal its dialectical vulnerability. It triggers an emotional reaction in the person hearing it, and thus masks the emotionalism of the person using it. Emotionalism about the subject of war has something noble, grand, and excusable about it and, better still, forms the basis for pacifism and humanitarianism. None the less, it is emotionalism that I think I recognize in Pierre Elliott Trudeau's thinking: that is, a personal attitude that is unequivocal and unyielding on a particular subject. This emotionalism is apparent in the second section, entitled "The Historical Approach," and it seems to be made up of two major components: first, faulty reasoning (that is, causality suggested between two entities that are really not comparable: nationalism and war),[10] and an over-emphasis of what, at this level of explanation, can only be a coin-cidence in which the actual degree of "interaction" is real but rather limited; and, secondly, an attitude based on a refusal to think about war and a desire to think only about peace. This "structural" scheme involves some obvious corollaries; for example, with war now threat-ening to become "international," peace should become "international-istic." A second corollary is that the overemphasis of organizing peace and avoiding war implies an underestimation of any particularity which, from this point of view, can only be conceived as a hindrance to the process of world-wide pacification and thus becomes a negative or at least "retrograde" factor. From this it is only a small step to say that evil (war) comes from fragmentation and good (world peace, universal disarmament) from internationalization; since nationalism and war are paired off at the beginning of the article, this step has already been taken in advance. The internationalism advocated by the author logi-cally demands the rejection of its principal opposite, nationalism, which is seen as a narrowing rather than a broadening movement.

In this framework, then, it is logical to link nationalism with regres-sive and almost malefic associations. The only extenuating considera-tion in this verdict is found in the notion of transition as applied to the nation-phenomenon: the qualities associated with nations "belong to a transitory period in world history."[11] If such is the case then nationalism can no longer be considered the cause of future wars. Logically, these two terms should be separated; it is even possible to consider certain forms of nationalism, particularly the most isolationist or insular ones, as political symptoms of a desire to escape from the interplay of force and power which degenerates into wars. And if there is transition, it must be in a direction which diminishes the nation because it is transi-tory, which implies that there is an existential "bonus" in the fact of not being transitory. Now, in relation to what are the realities of nation-hood or statehood transitory? What is the basis for comparison, and how is one reality superior to another? If it is a question of God, then that closes the discussion. But if this superior basis is the world or even the cosmos, who can say that these realities are not also transitory?

Transcendental Peace

In this context, pacifist thinking gives us an everyday example of the "internationalizing" dialectic:

> It is a commitment transcending any other commitments to one's native land, economic system or religion; countries, economic systems and religions are meaningful only if mankind is preserved. . . . Thus pacifists are not subject to shallow emotions or juvenile idealism: they submit to the most rigorous logic and attack the only problem whose solution must come before all others.[12]

If the world is in a state of emergency, as the pacifists see it, any activity not aimed at abating this fear is considered unimportant and, to go to extremes, laughable. This reasoning has often been explained: it consists in emphasizing the dangers of nuclear destruction and declaring any other vital investigation to be invalid. "Pacifist" anguish takes precedence over any other form of questioning.

In the name of a positive peace, any activity not geared to working for peace is finally ignored, which is tantamount to a premonitory annihilation of any problematic not connected with this state of emergency. Thus pacifism implicitly decides that any other problematic is unimportant; it annihilates all other philosophies *a priori*. In the name of a peace plan whose failure would be fatal for the world, we are incited to fear such a failure, the philosophic opposite of which is a detachment from everyday reality. This fear of atomic nothingness exclusively preoccupies those who sense it and counters all other commitments to reality, which, in view of the expected annihilation, become mere self-deception or, at best, a stay of execution.

Philosophical anguish feeds on everything. It is a mental attitude which consumes a great many symbols and justifications. It would be an error to see nothing but strictly political attitudes in the contemporary peace movements. For every man on earth, the "total" bomb poses the question of "the existence or annihilation of the world," extending to the whole cosmos the ancient doubts which in the past concerned only individual lives and which implicitly invested the rest of the world with unshakeable reality.

I too want peace, but I refuse in the name of the present political

climate to dismiss everything that is not central to this concern. Pacifism means fear of the bomb, and however effective this fear may be
politically, it contains a philosophical ambiguity.[13]

Now let us come back to nationalism.

Nations as Concepts

Should people stop making revolutions because they know that revolutions always pass, as they always—or almost always—have done?
Must we, in the name of vast federal or imperial political entities which
too will eventually be engulfed in the depths of time, must we dismiss
movements or revolutions which will, in the end, end? If nationalism in
any group—be it Senegalese or French-Canadian—is regressive, I still
believe that it is for reasons other than the immortality of the "French
Community" or the inherent superiority of a large grouping like Confederation over a small grouping like the state of Quebec. Is it perhaps
because nationalism causes war? I think the fragility of the correlation
between nationalism and war has already been proven. Is it then because nationalism tends irrevocably toward the socio-political right?
This presumes a future orientation based on political adventures of the
past, and nothing can make me believe that tomorrow's reality will be
like yesterday's or the day before yesterday's, which I agree were unfortunate. I no more believe in the predetermined characteristics of a
people than I do in those of an individual person; in politics, a doctrine
of predestination can lead only to immobility. Nations and peoples
have no essence. During a specific period of observation, they may display particular attitudes or institutions, but this is not their essence.
National groups are ontologically indeterminate, and this indetermination is the very foundation of their freedom. The future history of a human group is not fixed; it is unforeseeable. "A man is defined by his
plans," said Jean-Paul Sartre. The same is true for a people.

Should nationalism be condemned because it implies a movement
towards smaller communities at a time when the forces of History are
moving irreversibly towards internationalization? To that I would answer that the human race has supplied historians with a fine collection
of fallen empires: Alexander the Great, Genghis Khan, Solomon, Mo-
hammed, Franz Joseph, Hadrian, Caesar, and Victoria all proclaimed
the perpetuity of multiethnic and multicultural empires which in every

case have fallen into decline. If history with a capital "H" has a meaning, we may well learn that there is as much irrefutable evidence that this meaning is to be found in fragmentation as in planetary and worldwide integration. Nevertheless, I am still trying to discover why Trudeau considers nationalism, and more particularly its present separatist form in French Canada, as a seedbed for historical, social, human, and logical regression.

Is the nation-state a despicable trap into which the best elements of the left are stupidly lured by their emotions? Does the concept of the nation-state have a sort of malevolent and intrinsically negative essence that we should banish from our minds for ever and ever as one of the "transitory phases" of humanity which, like cannibalism, must be superseded? It is to this question that Pierre Elliott Trudeau proposes a brilliant reply that is rhetorically convincing, yet that seems to me to be a false question, or rather, a dialectical trap.

Let me explain. By postulating the premise that separatism assumes the establishment of a nation-state, it is relatively easy and even amusing to refute the aspirations of the French-Canadian people to becoming a nation-state. In point of fact, the concept of the nation-state is clearly outdated, corresponding neither to reality nor to the most recent scientific findings. The nation is not, as Trudeau suggests, an ethnic reality. Ethnic homogeneity no longer exists, or at least is very rare. Shifting population, immigration, assimilation (which Jacques Henripin quite rightly refers to as "linguistic transfers") have produced an intermingling of ethnic groups which has undeniably led, in French Canada for example, to regroupings that are no longer based on ethnic origin (or race, as it was still called twenty-five years ago) but rather on belonging to a homogeneous *cultural group*[14] whose only real common denominator is a linguistic one. One has simply to look around among one's personal acquaintances to count the number of true-blue French Canadians who are not "real" French Canadians: Mackay, Johnson, Elliott, Aquin, Molinari, O'Harley, Spénart, Esposito, Globenski, etc. . . . This says a lot about the French-Canadian ethnic-nation. The "linguistic transfers" referred to by Henripin have worked both for and against us, and the core of immigrant settlers that assured our survival has been long since mixed, ethnically speaking, with all the additions that immigration or flukes of love have brought to our national ethnic purity. In fact, the French-Canadian people has been replaced by a cultural-linguistic group whose common denominator is language. The same thing will happen to the Wolofs, Seres, and Fulani in Senegal who, if nothing interrupts the process of education and the resulting eventual formation of a cultural linguistic group of varied ethnic origin, will one day become Senegalese.

French Canada is polyethnic. And it would be pure folly, I agree, to dream of a nation-state for French Canada precisely at a time when the French-Canadian people has been succeeded by a culture that is total, coherent and differentiated by language. If this new conglomerate is to be called a nation, fine, but from then on there can be no question of the nation being a source of racism and all its abominable derivatives.

What distinguishes Canada from French Canada is not that the former is polyethnic and the latter monoethnic, but that the one is bicultural and the other culturally homogeneous (which, thank God, does not exclude pluralism in all its forms!).

The pairing of nation and state, against which Pierre Elliott Trudeau fulminates, no longer corresponds to reality; this fact in itself means that any minority which actually set this as its goal would never see its dreams fulfilled. It would be more precise to speak of a monocultural state. The few old fogeys who still dream of a pure French-Canadian race may simply be written off as intellectual delinquents! However, it seems to me unfair to argue against contemporary separatism by accusing it of racism and ethnic intolerance. It would be more appropriately studied as an expression of the culture of French Canadians seeking greater homogeneity.

From this perspective, and limiting ourselves strictly to the study of this phenomenon, nationalism *a priori* is a force neither for good nor for evil: it acts as a sort of collective voice that one is free to hear or to ignore. It may be opposed for reasons of political ideology, but not in the name of lucidity or knowledge. Besides, separatism may be seen as a particular form of *national presence*, but it is far from being the only one. Nationalism can be said to be the political expression of a culture; in the case of French Canada it is quite clearly the expression of political aspirations. Because of this, non-French Canadians see it as a constituent element of the French-speaking cultural group in Canada. In reality, proof of the existence of this cultural group can be seen in a variety of other forms: literature, the arts, the generalizing methodology of our researchers in the humanities, and surely also in our linguistic dynamism, demography, social struggles, religious peculiarities, and so on.

The Culture of Culture

We are thus looking at a culture which we shall call "national" and whose existence, however fragile, can be verified by a certain number of factors. French-Canadian separatism is only one of these factors, but it has a greater striking force than other forms of cultural existence because it contains the embryo of a revolution that could pose a threat to the present constitutional order in Canada. English Canadians have been quick to notice this and have hastened to isolate nationalism from all the other forms of cultural expression in French Canada. They have, for example, been generous and efficient in promoting the artistic peculiarity of French Canadians because this heightens the ambiguity of a connection which the separatists forcefully maintain is one-sided and "degrading." Patterning their behaviour on a number of well-known models in other parts of the world, English Canadians have invested a great deal of money and genuine interest in the "entertaining" aspects of French-Canadian culture. This has been accomplished so efficiently and so speedily that it has caused the beneficiaries to be mentally torn between their allegiance to a generous federal government and a not very profitable attachment to their own soil. The pettiness, intolerance, and political partisanship of the Duplessis regime caused this split to reach distressing proportions; many artists and intellectuals were thrown into the arms of the federal government, which meant that they were sentenced either to sterile anxiety or to becoming rootless spokesmen for a culture that had once appealed only to those who feared its full repercussions. One of the many consequences of this state of affairs was its influence on the Canadian use of the word *culture*.

Culture, in fact, has been restricted to the limited horizons of the arts and humanities; the word *culture* has contracted to the point where it now signifies only the artistic and cognitive characteristics of a group, whereas for anthropologists and many foreign intellectuals it describes the full range of behaviour patterns and symbols of a particular group and thus refers to a society that is sovereign and organic but not closed. The state of federal-provincial politics here has led us to depoliticize the word culture or, more precisely, to reject arbitrarily the comprehensive meaning conferred upon it by contemporary semantics. The Massey Report, with great precision, codified this reduction of French-Canadian culture to elements of cognition and artistic expression; coming at a time when great works of anthropology have established opposite connotations for the same word, it reveals a rejection of French-Canadian culture in its totality. It must be added that French-Canadian intellectuals immediately accepted this variant, and enthusiastically set about shaping their attitudes to conform with those of English Canada by urging upon French Canadians the merits and specialized practice of formalism, as if this would neutralize the propensity for exhibiting a total culture. Thus the problem is not to know whether we would be better poets in an independent state once the people are cleansed of the effects of a degrading political and emotional atmosphere, but to know whether the existence of French-Canadian culture is truly accepted or whether only a limited fragment of it is acknowledged, so that it can be included in a political conglomerate whose existence is considered a sort of priority.

A *complete* French-Canadian culture in no way presupposes any real homogeneity. No matter how dynamic a culture is, it is composed of a residue of indigenous and borrowed elements, the latter being at first heterogeneous and then gradually more or less assimilated and homogenized, until finally they are integrated into a total culture to the same extent as the original elements. This is true of French-Canadian culture, which has already been moulded by at least three spheres of cultural heterogeneity: French, British, and American.

> Because a culture is not merely a juxtaposition of cultural traits, there can be no such thing as a half-breed culture. . . . And for the same reason, one of the characteristics of culture is its style, a distinguishing mark that is peculiar to a people or period and which is evident in all areas of this people's activities at a given time. . . . One objection to this theory is that all cultures are a mixture of terribly heterogeneous elements. The case of Greek culture may be cited in this instance, being composed not only of Greek but also of Cretan, Egyptian, and Asiatic elements. . . . Heterogeneity is certainly the rule here. But beware: this heterogeneity is not experienced as such. . . . It is rather heterogeneity experienced from within as homogeneity. Heterogeneity may be quite apparent when the culture is analyzed, but however heterogeneous the elements may in fact be, they are experienced in the community consciousness as being just as much theirs as the most typically indigenous elements. What has taken place is a process of naturalization, which stems from the dialectic of possession.[15]

To be or not to be a separatist is a question of political choice and I can well imagine that French Canadians who see themselves as part of a total culture might still prefer to see their *culture* remain as part of Confederation rather than any other political regime. Besides, no one is forced into politics or even into political opinions; no one is compelled to commit himself to a political system that is conceived as a function of the totality of his culture. In theory, however, a rejection of the entirety of French-Canadian culture is implied by conceiving of it as part of a larger whole; from this point of view, separatism is no longer connected, relatively speaking, with the totality of French-Canadian culture, but has become only one aspect of it, opposed to Confederation, which makes it easy to suggest its narrowness as compared to the federal approach.

French-Canadian nationalism is the normal, if not predictable, expression of a culture whose comprehensiveness was being very subtly called into question at the same time as money was being provided for supposed compensations. Even before any value judgment is made about our sins, deficiencies, mistakes, or achievements, French Canada must be examined in the cold light of a culture which, whatever its shortcomings, is none the less total. On a rational level, this is much more important than worrying about whether separatism has died down in the past six months. One doesn't have to be a prophet to know that if French-Canadian culture exists, it will always have a tendency to reveal itself in its entirety and to break out of the limitations and "specializations" within which it has been "encapsulated." In a culture so oriented towards totality and homogeneity, this is an expression of a collective determination to survive.

Otherwise, French Canada is rejected as such and allowed to exist only in an *unchangeable* Confederation; this attitude may be likened to "*negative radicalism* as an affected inability to tolerate the slightest change in the regime."[16] Some mention must be made here of those who tell French-Canadian nationalists that all the "changes" they want are legal and possible within the framework of the constitution; this is a way of saying that it is possible to change everything except the political system:

By the terms of the existing Canadian constitution, that of 1867, French Canadians have all the powers they need to make Quebec a political society affording due respect for nationalist aspirations and at the same time giving unprecedented scope for human potential in the broadest sense.[17]

Our "Exceptional" Successes

Only the abolition of a total French-Canadian culture can enable Confederation to function smoothly and allow it to develop "normally" as a central power that reigns, not over two total cultures, but rather over ten administrative provinces. This abolition could come about in a variety of ways that would not prevent certain French-Canadian cultural stereotypes from surviving. By ceasing to be total, the culture of French Canada would enrich several spheres of Canadian life without any danger and without any political implications. We ourselves, just like our English-speaking partners, place a certain value on the survival of the folklore of the Amerindians. We have even cultivated a kind of snobbishness about the supposed drop of native blood in our veins, elegantly acknowledging our wild, instinctive, more remote origins! In our role as colonizers and conquerors, we naturally promote Eskimo art, Huron pottery, and the war chants of peoples whose culture has ceased to be total, no longer expressing a collective instinct for survival. As the attentions of the conquering majority become more and more sharply focused and full of concern, it becomes increasingly clear that they no longer fear the total expression of the minority culture.

In this respect, it must be recognized that English Canada has come very close to definitively mastering the situation, and may well still get the better of our *cultural fatigue*, which is very great. Each surge of nationalism catches English Canadians off guard, for they had thought, in good faith, that the problem was solved; then, after a period of hesitation and uncertainty, they take stock and decide that, after all, the minority's "nationalistic" outburst was well founded and that they must once again pay the price of harmony by making yet another concession. Or else (and this is an attitude that is common with certain French Canadians who follow the general trend of the fragmentation of French-Canadian culture), they take heart, saying that nationalism is like yellow fever and flares up periodically, in cycles.

The particularity of the majority position can be seen both in the sincerity and guilty conscience of the former attitude and in the theoretical exorcism of the eternally recurring nationalist "menstrual cycle" that characterizes the latter attitude. Domination is never unequivocal, except in detective films or westerns. The act of dominating (which is equivalent to having greater numbers or greater strength) eventually embarrasses those who dominate and pressures them into multiplying the ambiguities of the situation, which means that, because they have very guilty consciences, they do everything in their power to camouflage their dominant position. Sometimes the majority loses patience and ends up accusing the minority of counter-domination through foot-dragging and obstructionism that finally actually do occur. The minority, accused of being dead weights, assumes this role of villain more and more painfully. Actually, they *are* the villains, they are an obstacle, a ball and chain, an inert force whose demands and sensitivity constantly impede the progress of the dynamic majority; and they know it.[18]

Is it necessary, in this context, to catalogue all the psychological implications caused by the awareness of this minority position: self-punishment, masochism, a sense of unworthiness, "depression," the lack of enthusiasm and vigour—all the underlying reactions to dispossession that anthropologists refer to as "cultural fatigue"? French Canada is in a state of cultural fatigue and, because it is invariably tired, it becomes tiresome. Here we have a vicious circle. It would no doubt be much more relaxing to cease to exist as a *specific culture* and to sell our soul to English Canada once and for all for a Canada Council fellowship or a peaceful reservation protected by the RCMP. This cultural hypothesis, however, is no doubt impossible because of our numbers and also because of the unpredictable will to survive which we find sporadically and unevenly surging within each one of us.

A depoliticized French Canadian behaves like the member of a group that seems negligible in comparison to the infinite scope of the challenges facing it: God, world disarmament, hell and the atomic bomb, Confederation. This sublime unimportance is a path to mysticism and it creates an "order" which, like a sacrament, casts a pall of disrespectability on anyone who is not "set apart" by it. Nationalism, a profane impulse and practically considered a form of juvenile sacrilege, thus becomes a sin that more or less stigmatizes anyone who advocates it even temporarily. It is a form of adolescent impulsiveness that can be forgiven when those who have succumbed to it later reconsider in the serenity or repentance of maturity. This impulsive and "verbal" expression of nationalism is tolerated and is seldom loudly condemned, which explains how in French Canada it has become a kind of cathartic melodrama. Its very toleration is an effective form of subordination whereby nationalism is made into a kind of sinful excess built into the system it is incoherently trying to overthrow, but which it never really disturbs. It is all right to be a nationalist—for a while, as in the thankless years of one's adolescence—so long as you eventually get back to more serious matters, back to reality.

At first, nationalism comes as a surprise, like a teenage son's first acts of rebellion; later it starts to be viewed with concern, not only by the Federalists but by French Canadians exhausted from thinking of the effort it would take to live outside the system of acceptance and grandeur proposed by their leaders, those disciples of understanding, unity, and vast entities, spokesmen for the great urgent problems facing the world, and for religion. This system (has it occurred to anyone that it might not be more coherent than any other!) has worked well for a long time and in no way threatens the existence of the French fact in Canada; it means simply that this French fact must be domesticated at all levels and in every conscience. Just how effective this attitude is can be seen by its pervasiveness in French Canada, where we find its greatest advocates. Speaking in French, their voices packed with emotion, they easily convince their fellow citizens that remaining French Canadian is the only way, repeating the old adage that "it's up to us to make ourselves felt, for only by being better can we show English Canada how dynamic French-Canadian culture is."

If Quebec became such a shining example, if to live there were to partake of freedom and progress, if culture enjoyed a place of honour there, if the universities commanded respect and renown from afar, if the administration of public affairs were the best in the land (and none of this presupposes any declaration of independence!) French Canadians would no longer need to do battle for bilingualism; the ability to speak French would become a status symbol, even an open sesame in business and public life. Even in Ottawa, superior competence on the part of our politicians and civil servants would bring spectacular changes.[19]

The logic of the system seems unwittingly subservient to its own ends. It is hardly necessary to point out here the no doubt unconscious attempt to "dis-effect" French Canada in its totality. Anyone who wants to get ahead must reject the cultural impetus given him by French Canada and start from a position of cultural fatigue; this is like having a devil inside him, which he himself must kill just to prove that, through him, French Canada has a right to exist! But we forget that this can happen only in exceptional cases, and that therefore only the individual is important, for the culture he represents is, by implication, diminished by the "exceptional" nature of his success: "[. . .] personal, localized success tends to posit itself for itself as an essential moment all the more when common success seems compromised or more distant."[20]

Total "Functionarization"

Why should French Canadians have to be better? Why should they have to "get ahead" to justify their existence? This exhortation to *individual* superiority is presented as a challenge that must absolutely be answered. We should not forget, however, that a cult of challenges depends on an initial obstacle or handicap and that it finally boils down to a test of strength to which each individual is subjected. Only the achievement counts, and strictly according to this criterion, we would have to concede that Maurice Richard was more successful than our federal politicians. We have a sportsman's attitude to national affairs, and by dreaming of creating heroes rather than a state, we force ourselves as individuals to win struggles that are really collective.

If the individual challenge that every French Canadian tries in vain to take up depends on the position of the French-Canadian group as a whole, why should this collective challenge be taken as if it were an individual one? Would it not be more logical to respond collectively to collective challenges and to cope totally with the total threats that are built into French Canada's position vis-à-vis her English-speaking federalist partners in Confederation?

"If Canada as a state has had so little room for French Canadians," writes Trudeau, "it is above all because we have failed to make ourselves indispensable to its future."[21] Making ourselves indispensable to the destiny of others! Here we see the theme of cultural exorbitation expressed with rare precision. It consists in creating in the majority group a need for the minority, an "indispensability" which immediately confers upon us the right to the dignity of a minority; thus, in the scheme proposed by Pierre Elliott Trudeau (and which is familiar to all consumers of federalist French-Canadian thinking), the minority group would fully and dynamically occupy the "little bit of space" it now has, or would play a much larger role if it earned it. In other words, the existence of the French-Canadian group can only be justified if it remains grafted onto an English-speaking majority which can no longer get along without it. At the end of this brave new world, French Canada would have a better place in the federal state, but it would always be only one place; that is, it would play a larger or more fitting "role." But this role, however large or small, will always be only one role: its political trajectory would be shaped from the start by the consenting majority, and it would remain part of an entity into which it would have to fit harmoniously. In this scenario, French Canada would play a role, sometimes even a starring role, in a story it could never write itself. [22]

This glorious and heroic future, however, is strangely reminiscent of our past. As long as it has been held within the confines of a structure it never invented, French Canada has played a "role" in federal affairs, courageously, brilliantly, or wearily filling in a space for which it was never really fitted. It could have done better, of course, but a civil servant is not a cabinet minister: he is less involved in the business, tires quickly, is not so keen, is a bit wary, and can often be found thinking about his retirement. Now, if I may be excused for making a scholastic analogy, French Canada on the whole is like a collective civil servant; it finds itself on the payroll of great employers who are resolute and just—the federal government and the Catholic Church. In choosing functionarization rather than totalization, the French Canadian enjoys all the benefits that come with the position (salary, status, security, promotion) and has no other responsibilities or inconveniences except those inherent in the subordination of all functions to the organism. Faithful to the terms of the contract, and grateful for all the comforts of paternalism, French Canada is collectively a civil servant who never causes any "trouble" and never resents his bosses. A civil servant is neither an entrepreneur nor a politician. And it seems to me that there is a link between our lack of entrepreneurs, which in the past was considered a racial deficiency, and our total, continuous conscription by large employers: the federal government which protects us from ourselves (read "Duplessis") and the Church, which for a long time acted as a substitute government for us, to such an extent that French Canada has an abundance of religious institutions and numerous clergy who work efficiently, but who, conversely, do not offer a good example of either faith or holiness.

French Canada as such is a good public servant and its behaviour in this sense abounds in signs that are far more convincing than any analogies can suggest: identification with the bosses, desire for promotion, very noticeable social conformity (calling it low profile is an understatement!), marked talent for being agreeable, general desire to raise its standard of living, and to end my comparison on a cruel note, full integration into the system of which it is only a function. In this way our representatives in Ottawa are elected as "MPs" but become civil servants as soon as they reach good old Parliament Hill. And here they are in a perfect conundrum: they are the people's elected representatives but, with rare exceptions, can conceive of themselves only as functionaries because they represent a functionarized people!

Eccentricity

Traditionally, the key to success for French Canada has been to look outward, toward a heterogeneous culture. Our MPs in Ottawa and our writers in France, by seeking their mission and fulfilment elsewhere, have thus saddled themselves with such an enormous handicap that they are condemned to a single form of action and success: apotheosis. In both cases their valiant exiles have also meant demoralizing reversals. The breakthrough in Ottawa and recognition in Paris have led to sacrifices that are fruitless, if not downright overwhelming. The loss of one's roots—an endless source of cultural fatigue—or exile, renunciation, and removal from one's own element, can never completely free the individual from his original identity, yet at the same time they prevent him from fully identifying with his new surroundings. He is a double expatriate, cut off from both cultural sources and twice deprived of a homeland. This voluntary and eventually fatal orphanhood, even if not reflected in consular irregularities, eats away at him like a tapeworm. Setting down roots, on the other hand, is to take constant, secret, and ultimately fulfilling nourishment from the original soil.

Tell me that Joyce wrote *Ulysses* because of his exile and I will answer that, precisely, Joyce only found a meaning to his exile by poetically "going home." For him, Trieste, Paris, and Zurich were simply nostalgic springboards which he used, in a mental process that eventually ended in delirium, to effect a daily, hour-by-hour return to his dreary Ireland. That he was buried outside his isle in a Swiss cemetery strikes one as an accident, especially considering that his entire work is a brilliant resurrection of the Ireland he never saw again, and which, with his dimmed eyes, he could never have seen again even if he had returned. He brought his native land to life in books that are as extravagant as his obsessions. One might even wonder whether the almost incomprehensible English in which *Finnegans Wake* was composed during his "blindness" was not a final revolutionary act by this exiled writer who, from the time of his youth in Dublin, was already exiled by the language that had become the "mother tongue" there: English, historically a "foreign" language.

Perhaps it was not so much his own country that he fled so rapidly, but rather his own language, which he was disowning by speaking it. He fled the English language through those "foreign" languages that he taught for Berlitz, thus clinging to anything "foreign" (non-British) in the English tongue. Condemned to speak a foreign language, he took his mysterious revenge by making it foreign unto itself. After conquering it completely and investing it with universal semantic overtones, he set about disarticulating it to the point of incoherence; he expressed it so thoroughly that finally, in an exploded language bordering on the incommunicable, he was able to describe a painful and passionate experience of setting down roots. The deliberate use of Gaelic, which he thought a ridiculous project, could impress him only as chauvinism—the very proof that his own culture had been reduced to folklore. Taking a language that was both foreign and his 'mother' tongue, he chose rather to exhaust it by wildly inflating its meanings, contradictions, origins, and derivations, so that out of this magical, irresistible torrent of "uprooted" words there emerges his native Ireland, thoroughly contaminated by the cross-breeding of words, tragic, laughable, unsure, loved, hated, and defunct: a motherland regained, yet still somehow unattainable.

Besides—and here I am trying to refute the claims that Joyce's experience was exceptional—Faulkner, Balzac, Flaubert, Baudelaire, Mallarmé, and Goethe all produced works that are universal because they are so rooted in the countries in which they were written. As one's self-identification becomes clearer, one becomes better at communicating it, for expression comes from deep within the self. Understanding does not result from an initial, deliberate depersonalization of the speaker;

on the contrary, dialogue is enriched to the extent that both partici-pants are profoundly and particularly themselves.

In this regard, French-Canadian literature is distressingly poor. In far too many cases our authors have opted to leave their own "native element" and have systematized this rejection, hoping thus to attain universality. Other "regional" authors have opted for "folkloric au-thenticity," and because they have managed to flog some mileage out of the local scene, or simply because of their mediocrity, they think of themselves as being more French Canadian. An author can't come to terms with his origins simply by adding a few bits of local colour that would be more obvious to reporters from the Parisian magazine *Marie-Claire* than they are to us. Some authors think that just because they spice up a familiar sentence with a few curses they have given a literary existence to their birthplace. This is sad, because in their thirst for the exotic they end up seeing themselves through the eyes of foreigners who come to spend a couple of weeks in Quebec. That which is typical is profound and should not be confused with either superficial stereo-types or regionalism, which to my mind is rooted only in its localism. The problem is not to write stories that take place in Canada, but to as-sume all the difficulties of one's identity fully and painfully. French Can-ada, like Fontenelle on his deathbed, feels "a certain difficulty in be-ing."

Our federal politicians, having taken the first step towards becom-ing part of a great "whole," are in a continual state of emotional exile which, incidentally, prevents them from being aware of the strains of their situation. They are procrastinators by profession, always telling us about a Confederation which in fact does not exist. It is a condi-tioned reflex: how could they sincerely root themselves in French Can-ada when, politically, by their very presence in the federal government, they have shown themselves ready to sacrifice it to appease the stronger? Traitors? No! Our federalists are sincere, hence their am-biguity.

The French Canadian is both literally and figuratively a double agent. He wallows in "eccentricity," and in his fatigue longs to reach political nirvana through self-dissolution. The French Canadian rejects his centre of gravity, desperately searching for a centre elsewhere and wandering through any labyrinth he comes across. He is neither preyed upon nor persecuted, yet he always leaves his country behind in a con-tinual search for exoticism that never satisfies him. Homesickness is both the need for and rejection of a cultural matrix. All these transcendental impulses towards great political, religious, or cosmological entities can never replace the need to put down roots; as complementary processes, they could have an enriching influence, but by themselves these impulses turn French Canadians into "displaced persons."

I myself am one of these "typical" men, lost, unsettled, tired of my atavistic identity and yet condemned to it. How many times have I rejected the immediate reality of my own culture? I wanted total expatriation without suffering, I wanted to be a stranger to myself, I used to reject all the very surroundings I have finally come to affirm. Today I tend to think that our cultural existence can be something other than a perpetual challenge, and that the fatigue can come to an end. This cultural fatigue is a fact, a disquieting, painful reality, but it may also be the path to immanence. One day we will emerge from the struggle, victorious or vanquished. One thing is certain: the inner struggle goes on, like a personal civil war, and it is impossible to be either indifferent or serene about it. The struggle, though not its outcome, is fatal.

Culturally fatigued and weary, French Canada for a long time now has been going through an endless winter; every time the sun breaks through the ceiling of cloud that has obliterated the heavens, in spite of our weakness, our sickness and disillusionment, we start hoping for spring again. French-Canadian culture has long been dying; it makes frequent recoveries, followed by new relapses, and thus leads a precarious existence of fits, starts, and collapses.

What will finally become of French Canada? To tell the truth, no one really knows, especially not French Canadians, whose ambivalence on this subject is typical: they want simultaneously to give in to cultural fatigue and to overcome it, calling for renunciation and determination in the same breath. If anyone needs to be convinced of this, he need only read the articles our great nationalists have written—profoundly ambiguous speeches in which one can scarcely distinguish exhortations to revolt from appeals for constitutionality, revolutionary ardour from willed obedience. French-Canadian culture shows all the symptoms of extreme fatigue, wanting both rest and strength at the same time, desiring both existential intensity and suicide, seeking both independence and dependency.

Independence can only be considered as a social and political expedient in a relatively homogeneous culture. It is not historically necessary, any more than the culture that calls for it is. It should not be seen as a superior, preferential form of existence for a cultural community.

One thing is sure, however: independence is just as valid a form of cultural existence as dependence. From an intellectual point of view, the forms of existence for any given cultural group are equally interesting. Knowledge is concerned with realities, not values.

Dialectic Fatigue

> The struggle is... intelligibility itself.
> Jean-Paul Sartre[23]

If the presence of tension is inherent to dialectics, and if dialectics opposes two opposite extremities which are progressively revealed to one another, then it would be a dialectical error to deny the fact that Canada is a well-defined dialectical case in which two cultures confront one another. If one wishes to reach an understanding of the Canadian situation, it is more logical to consider it in the framework of a critical opposition of two cultures than to dismantle, by over-valuing the superior term of reference, the historical dialectic of which French Canada is a part. A logical dismantling of the dialectic amounts to saying "French Canada is very small compared to reality X... and its totality becomes simply a particularity in this new scale of size." For example, French Canada can be crushed dialectically by making the point of comparison either the huge, invading bulk of America, or the threat of world-wide atomic war, or the urgent need for universal disarmament, or the universality of the Catholic religion, or world socialism, etc.... Our ideologists frequently make overwhelming comparisons between our culture and remote, ideal considerations; in practical terms, this reveals a desire to see French-Canadian culture as a "diminished" entity. The great considerations advanced by our intellectuals are not without importance or significance, but they are distinguished, in the French-Canadian context, by a lesser degree of dialectical action upon its culture. The presence of these great considerations acts against the interests of French Canada; caught in a crushing comparison, French Canada must feel tremendous guilt simply for existing while these enormous problems remain to be faced.

Another means of diminishing French Canada is to accept it only in its administrative interpretation as a province. "Quebec is a province like the others" boils down to accepting the reality of French-Canadian culture only in the legalistic terms of Confederation, thus regionalizing and provincializing the culture. This reasoning is the inverse of the other in terms of the size of the opposing term of reference, but structurally it is similar in that it circumvents the French Canada/English Canada axis, which is the most significant (historically and politically), but which of course does not exclude French Canada's multidimensional relations with both the world and history.

On the whole, our intellectuals have repeatedly rejected the historical dialectic by which we are defined and have turned to another dialectic which, in widening the confrontation or narrowing it excessively, shows a refusal to consider French Canada as a total culture. This repudiation has formed the ideological basis for several systems of thought in Canada. Our intellectuals have deployed a vast logical arsenal to escape from the French-Canadian dialectic, a situation which even today is exhausting, depressing, and degrading for French Canada. "How to get out of it" has been the basic problem for our intellectuals, and their dialectical escapes only give tragic expression to the morbid taste for exile that has been prevalent in our literature since the time of Crémazie. What they have been fleeing, whether by writing ideological rubbish or by travelling, is an intolerable position of subordination, disgust with themselves and their people, bitterness, unrelenting fatigue, and a firm intent not to undertake anything more. French Canadians are often represented by their most prominent spokesmen as a jaded people who believe neither in themselves nor in anything else. Self-devaluation has done its work for a long time now, and if only one proof were to be given, I would mention the delirious exaggeration indulged in by French-Canadian separatists. Although they do puff themselves up, it must be said in their defence that if they did not do so, conditioned as they are to collapse and defeat, they would probably have to take themselves for absolute idiots, an idea which is constantly being reinforced by the society around them.

French Canada, a dying, tired culture, is at square one in politics. Those who have been most successful politically are "a-nationalists." They are the ones who have best "represented" this unrealized, parcelled, and dispossessed people. Success for our federal politicians has depended on their cultural "dis-integration." Their "inexistence" has reflected the constrained culture they represent and which they have almost all been eager to "fatigue" even more by turning it into folklore so successfully that the federal government, by its very existence, proclaims that there is no longer any dialectical tension between the French- and English-Canadian cultures. The federal government is not the focus of a basic, elemental struggle; in fact it has never been so, or very rarely. The federal superstructure, in sanctifying the political appeasement of French Canada, does not stem from the historical dialectic of the two Canadas, but from a desire to suppress this dialectic, so that Ottawa, a capital between two provinces, rules over ten of them. The political portrait of Canada masks the real confrontation between two cultures and glosses over this confrontation in a disguised monolithic regime which legalistically considers French Canada to be one province out of ten. The dialectical struggle between the two Canadas does not take place in Ottawa; it is "depoliticized," at least in the sense that there are no "institutions" either resulting from it or containing it. The dialectical struggle is in fact taking place elsewhere, almost everywhere, and deep within our consciousness as well. It is not for us to say how it will end, but it is important to know that it is going on and becoming more and more unavoidable. Fatigue, however great, is still not death.

Universalism

I will have been misunderstood if in the course of this article I have been taken to be disparaging *universalism* in my attempt to re-establish the reality of "transitory" phases of History and to underline the importance of one's own culture and the "national fact."[24]

Universalism should in no way evoke supremacies of ancient empires, and must never be built on the corpses of "national" cultures any more than of men. I sincerely believe that humanity is involved in a process of convergence and unification. But this project of *unanimization*, as described by Senghor after Teilhard de Chardin, must, in order to be successful, resemble a project of love and not one of bitter fusion in a forced and sterile totalization. The dialectic of opposition must become a dialectic of love. Universal harmony must not be achieved at the cost of ignoring either the *person* or the *"human branches."*

May I be permitted here to quote Teilhard de Chardin, whose thinking I feel adequately expresses this ultimate reconciliation of the general and the particular, the "indigenous" and the "universal":

Love has always been carefully eliminated from realist and positivist concepts of the world; but sooner or later we shall have to acknowledge that it is the fundamental impulse of Life, or, if you prefer, the one natural medium in which the rising course of evolution can proceed. . . . It links those who love in bonds that unite but do not confound, causing them to discover in their mutual contact an exaltation capable, incomparably more than any arrogance of solitude, of arousing in the heart of their being all that they possess of uniqueness and creative power. . . . Union differentiates, as I have said; the first result being that it endows a convergent Universe with the power to extend the individual fibres that compose it without their being lost in the whole. . . . In other words, in a converging Universe each element achieves completeness, not directly in a separate consummation, but by incorporation in a higher pole of consciousness in which alone it can enter into contact with all others. By a sort of inward turn towards the Other its growth culminates in an act of giving and in excentration.[25]

Union, if you wish, but between entities which accord each other mutual recognition. The planetary union to which Teilhard de Chardin refers can mean neither the constitutional rule of more powerful elements over a group which has virtually *ceased to exist*, nor domination by an external legal body over its constituent parts. To return to Teilhard de Chardin: "A total earth requires nations that are fully aware." This formula seems to me more a basic prerequisite for convergence than an expression of fervent universalism seeking to prove itself even at the expense of all the lives it intends to transform, but not of the individual *super-being* without which a desire for unity would be futile.

Continued and irreversible progress is perhaps real, but it is so vast in scope and in such huge measures of human time that no one revolution can dogmatically decree that others which do not seem to be continuing it are superfluous or superseded. Who could claim to have advanced humanity so much that initiatives unforeseen by him would necessarily be steps backwards? No one has a sure monopoly on revolution, and consequently no one has the right to condemn divergent revolutions or those on a different path. "Ideally," writes Roland Barthes, "revolution being an essence that is at home everywhere, it is logical and necessary at any point in the unfolding of time."[26]

["La fatigue culturelle du Canada français."
Liberté IV, no. 23 (May 1962): 299–325.]

Notes

Most of the notes to this essay are Aquin's own. Where I have made significant changes or additions, other than supplying references to English translations of works cited wherever possible, this is indicated in parentheses after the note. (*Ed.*)

1. Aquin's reference is to Vol. 5 (*L'Avenir de l'homme*), p. 74 of Teilhard de Chardin's *Oeuvres*. I have been unable to find the passage in question. (*Ed.*)

2. Pierre Elliott Trudeau, "La nouvelle trahison des clercs," *Cité Libre* 46 (April 1962), pp. 3–16. Reprinted in translation in Pierre Elliott Trudeau, *Federalism and the French Canadians*, trans. Patricia Claxton (Toronto: Macmillan, 1968), pp. 151–81. All subsequent references will be to Claxton's translation.

3. Trudeau, pp. 157–58.

4. The "nationalistic" wars of the nineteenth century are sometimes attributed, by going back through the series of "causes," to the Congress of Vienna in 1815, the first "summit meeting" for peace: "At Vienna, the map of Europe was remade, but freedom, national spirit and the rights of national groups were all ignored in this restructuration. In the final act of Vienna were sown the seeds of wars which would bathe the second half of the nineteenth century in blood. The repression of various national groups accentuated the strife beteen governments and peoples." Félix Ponteil, *L'Éveil des nationalités et le mouvement libéral* (Paris: PUF, 1960), p. 4.

5. "Professor Wright notes that between 1482 and 1941, that is between the Treaty of Arras, which sanctioned Louis XI's victories and in effect marked the end of feudalism, and the United States' entry into the Second World War, it is possible to count 278 wars and 700 million casualties." General Gallois, quoted by Louis Armand in *Plaidoyer pour l'avenir* (Paris: Calman-Lévy, 1961), p. 146.

6. Pierre Elliott Trudeau also mentions modern technology as an external cause of war. On this point he makes a causal inversion. The correlation between war and technology seems to me to work in the opposite direction: surely it is warfare which has created its tools, and not the other way around. Conversely, however, tools of war must have had an effect on perfecting or extending methods of destruction; but it would be difficult to put all the blame on technological progress, which on a functional level can be useful as well as destructive. The same, after all, is true of fire.

7. I found the following phrase in Teilhard de Chardin: "true peace... betokens neither the ending nor the reverse of warfare, but war in a naturally sublimated form." Teilhard de Chardin, *The Future of Man*, trans. Norman Denny (London: Collins, New York: Harper & Row, 1964), p. 153.

8. Claude Lévi-Strauss, *Conversations with Claude Lévi-Strauss*, trans. John and Doreen Weightman (London: Jonathan Cape, 1969), pp. 41–42 & [33].

9. Aquin's reference is to Cheikh Anta Diop, *Présence Africaine* 24–25 (February-May 1959), p. 376. The passage quoted does not appear there, and while there is an article by Diop in the issue ("L'unité culturelle africaine," pp. 60–65), it has no real bearing on the idea expressed in the quotation. (*Ed.*)

10. Aquin quotes Trudeau at this point: "Le concept de nation... c'est un concept qui pourrit tout." However, the quotation misleads by omission; the Claxton translation of the full passage reads as follows: "A concept of nation that pays so little honour to science and culture obviously can find no room above itself in its scale of values for truth, liberty, and life itself. It is a concept that corrupts all... " (p. 157). (*Ed.*)

11. Ibid., p. 177.
12. André Langevin, "Einstein and Peace," *Le Nouveau Journal*, Montreal, April 1962.
13. "[T]his terror of inevitable war, which sees no cure for warfare except in even greater terror, is responsible for poisoning the air we breathe." *The Future of Man*, p. 149.
14. The notion of culture, according to E.B. Tylor, is "that complex whole which includes knowledge, belief, art, morals, laws, custom, and any other capabilities and habits acquired by man as a member of society." Edward B. Tylor, *Primitive Culture* (London: John Murray, 1871) vol. I, p. 1. A more recent source, Claude Lévi-Strauss, specifies: "Language is at once the prototype of the cultural phenomenon whereby all the forms of social life are established and perpetuated." *Structural Anthropology*, trans. Claire Jacobson and B.G. Schoepf (New York: Basic Books, 1963), pp. 358–59.
15. Aimé Césaire, "Culture et colonisation." Lecture delivered at the Sorbonne, September 1956.
16. Jean-Paul Sartre, *Critique of Dialectical Reason*, trans. Alan Sheridan-Smith (London: NLB, 1976), vol. I, p. 768.
17. Trudeau, p. 180.
18. "[. . .] a people's mental image of itself is no less a stereotype than its mental images of other peoples, for it is arrived at by the same irrational, arbitrary and irresponsible methods." Jean Stoetzel, *Without the Chrysanthemum and the Sword. A Study of the Attitudes of Youth in Post-War Japan* (New York: Columbia University Press, Unesco Publication, 1955), p. 15.
19. Trudeau, p. 180.
20. Sartre, p. 589.
21. Trudeau, p. 166.
22. Lord Durham was right, in this sense, when he wrote that French Canadians were a people without history! (History obviously belonged to English Canadians, and all we could do was to take it as one takes a train.) If we agree to play a role, however noble, it has to be in a history written by others. It is impossible to be both a function and the organism controlling it, a "role-playing" cultural entity and an historic totality. I am using the word "history" here in an Hegelian sense, which is also the way the *Montreal Star* uses it ("History in the making"). As for historical science, that's something else. We have a history, but it interests no one but us, unfortunately.
23. Sartre, p. 816.
24. "Marx minimized the national fact. The nationalism of new, coloured states proved him wrong. But where nationalists want only to see racial, religious, political or social phenomena, Teilhard de Chardin distinguishes an 'ethnico-politico-cultural' synthesis. He concludes: 'The *natural unity* into which humanity subdivides is not therefore either the anthropologists' single race, or the sociologists' single nations or cultures: it is a certain amalgam of the two, which, for want of a better term I will henceforth call the *branch of humanity*.' [Teilhard de Chardin, *The Vision of the Past*, trans. J.M. Cohen (London: Collins, New York: Harper & Row, 1966), p. 201.] And for which I would give the example of France." Léopold Sédar Senghor, *Pierre Teilhard de Chardin et la politique africaine* (Paris: Seuil, 1962), p. 49.
25. *The Future of Man*, pp. 54–56.
26. Roland Barthes, *Michelet par lui-même* (Paris: Seuil, 1954), p. 55.

Occupation: Writer

Since receiving confirmation through the passport office of my appointment to holy orders, I have committed one sacrilege after another against my official calling. It has got to the point where there is a certain pleasure in cheating on my vocation and even in refusing systematically and categorically to think of myself as a writer. However, my insistence that I am no longer a purveyor of words has not blinded me to the fact that I have never abandoned the hypocritical desire to rock my paying public with a comeback all the more sensational for being unheralded. But in the time that it takes to change profession (other than on my passport), I have had to face the fact that, as far as the people I deal with are concerned, my past activities define me forever as a man of letters. A few commissions, a seemingly irreversible induction into the Society of Authors—that is all it takes to remind me that from now on, despite my denials and divagations, I am enmeshed in the ungreased wheels of a machinery which puts me back in my place.

A most vicious circle, this socio-biographical circuit of mine! I have put it to the test and returned in dismay to writing like a mailman delivering mail. I feel like a Jew whose Jewishness comes from the way other people see him. I wear it like a scar, writ large on my face. Never have I felt less like a writer, yet still I go on writing. But if luck or laziness do not force me out of my official writer's residence, I intend to take Her Majesty my half-dead language and make her pay dearly for my syntactic incarceration and the stranglehold she has on me. That's right; I plan to take my revenge on the quicksilver words for this fine career opening before me like a mineshaft ready to swallow up whoever ventures in to dig. I am prey to destructive impulses against this wretched French language which, for all its majesty, still comes second. Writing kills me. I do not want to go on writing, to go on juggling with Hamlet's "words, words, words," trying to give clear expression to the unimaginable, planning the details of the premeditated verbal crime, looking for a black cat in a dark room, especially when it is not there. . . . But why, you may well ask, having said all this, am I now writing these easily refutable thoughts? To tell the truth, I hardly know myself and am inclined to think of my being drafted by *Parti pris*[1] as rather like being involved in an accident. And, after all, I have every right to lapse into illogicality once I give up the pretence of any semiotic mission. In this flaming bordello of a country in pieces, writing is like saying one's prayers while sitting on a nitroglycerine bomb set to explode in five minutes time. It's a free country and I am sure that I can invoke if necessary the right of any citizen to write his own breviary when the mood takes him.

There are those who will think that I am as nutty as a fruit cake and that my refusal to write can be explained in terms of my neuroses. While I shall not change any minds amongst those readers, whose opinions are quite sincere, I remain none the less convinced that, in rising up like an Antichrist from the riotous growth of words on the blank page, I am in full control of what I am doing: I am making a conscious choice, responding in the process to a particular historical challenge. In December 1963, in this latency period and in our province's state of unrest, with Paul Comtois as Lieutenant Governor of Galilee[2] and me being what I am, I do solemnly swear that fine intellectual works and novels good for the Governor General's invariably promote the notion that literature is a function of the organic unity of our nation. Well, we are dis-organized, so you can draw your own conclusions.

And then, if we are to be perfectly honest, the originality of a piece of work is directly proportional to the ignorance of its readers. There is no originality: works of literature are reproductions (which serve a purpose of course in a society with large amounts of spare time to kill and blessed, moreover, with pulp) run off from worn out plates made from other "originals" reproduced from reproductions that are true copies of earlier forgeries that one does not need to have known to understand that they were not archetypes but simply variants. A cruel invariability governs the mass production of those variants that go by the name of original works. History, too, copies itself. Originality is as impossible there as in literature. Originality does not exist; it is a delusion. Fashion alone creates the illusion of difference: fashion in the sense of the filmy veil, the deceptively diaphanous surface, the clothes which permit distinctions where none exist. A few insignificant details are all that differentiate me from a sick Hungarian who might have set out, one evening in May, to write an article in an attempt to exorcize his cephalomanic fatigue. Around 1913 our man would probably have worn a double-breasted jacket and a detachable collar; unable to write in front of a small television screen, he probably blackened his Austrian-made paper while drinking a German beer at the Café Mozart.

These few differences are minor and cannot hide our sad resemblance, the national syphilis that so implacably unites us, the pain of seeing who we are in a world in which politeness means putting ourselves in parentheses and preservation means putting ourselves in bottles. Unfortunately, Freud did not attempt the psychoanalysis of what it was to be Hungarian in a proud Vienna defined by its determination to repress the Hungarians who lived there, with their bad minority breath and their music which it was convenient to confuse with that of the gypsies—all of which shows only too clearly the willingness of the Viennese to see their partners in history as nothing but nomads. It would seem that, in any situation of ethnic domination, it is the inferior group that is the more musical of the two: the Hungarians whose musicality was much vaunted by their masters, the American Negroes, even the French Canadians who are cast as gypsies in relation to the dominant group which acts as a sedentary public. The domination of one human group by another places an exaggerated importance on those powers of the inferior group which are harmless: sex, artistic proclivities, natural talent for music or creation, and so on. Are we not, as French Canadians, interested in Eskimo art and in the mythology of the

Indians we keep on reservations? That is the blind compensation of the dominated: the knowledge that below them there exists a group that allows them to display their own dominance with a perfectly clear conscience.

Is the fact that I am artistically gifted of any importance? No, but it is important to realize that my artistic gifts derive from the very fact that I am dominated, that my entire people is dominated, and that their masters like them that way: singing gypsies, artists to the tips of their fingers, naturally inclined toward those social activities which pay the least. At bottom, I refuse to write works of art, after years of conditioning in that direction, because I refuse the significance that art assumes in an ambiguous world. As an artist, I would be playing a part that had been assigned to me: that of a talented underling. Well, I refuse this talent, uncertainly perhaps, because I refuse everything that has to do with my domination. Which is as good as saying that, if I go on with this article I am writing, I shall do my utmost to put into it everything that should not be there in the article expected of me. By pursuing this undertaking without enthusiasm, I am trying to draw attention to my artistic shortcomings and demonstrate by my ramblings that domination no longer has any effect on me, that I have no taste either for the security or the historical insignificance it bestows, and that I will fight it by any means I can so long as they have shock value.

The good little French Canadian, destined for a brilliant if frivolous future, suddenly takes it upon himself to produce a piece of writing governed by the thematics of the refusal to write—a meaningless gesture which might acquire significance only by the simultaneous explosion of all the sticks of dynamite which now lie rotting in the arsenals of the Province of Quebec. Explosions have serious disadvantages, one of which is the shattering of all historical structures situated within a given radius of the shockwave. The internal structure of any literary project has to be detectable, even if it takes the form of a literary anti-structure as is the case with Robbe-Grillet. Thus, destructuring is just another way of structuring if it concerns the same sphere of activity, such as literature. Now in my case, if the structures are shattered by the impact of the explosion within me, it is not so that they can be replaced by a literary counter-structure, but so that there will be no place left at all for a literature which, were I to give in to its charms, would express nothing but my own internalization of two centuries of domination. A lame excuse, it might be said, to hide a simple lack of talent. But

such an objection, which involves a change of level and is hence irrefutable, does not affect me; for here, according to the logic of domination, even a lack of talent might be seen as a display of bad temper on
the part of the dominated who, without really knowing why, refuses to
have anything to do with a vocation which he believes to be personal
but which is really historical, in the same way that the talent of the
dominated derives from the desire to effect in some way in art the revolution of which he is incapable in history.

By dissociating myself from literature in this way, I am writing myself off, ensuring in advance that anything I do write will be denounced
as the unfaithful expression of my refusal to write. Now, what characterizes literary works is the formal necessity—or urgency—invoked by
their authors. Despite their repeated protestations of non-formalism,
writers cannot escape being formalists in the sense that their very existence is defined by the forms they use and which establish their uniqueness as authors. Outside literature proper, the form of written works
becomes secondary, unimportant, often chosen according to circumstances or, as is my case now, not chosen at all and not wanted. What
matters to me is something quite different, something which is beyond
literature without being a metaliterature or an old ambition in a new
guise; something which involves the destruction of the historical conditioning which has led me to internalize my domination. In rejecting
domination I refuse literature, the daily bread of the dominated who
are allowed to enjoy a monopoly in the manufacture of symbols, leading inevitably to overproduction. Has it not been established that
colonized countries invariably produce excessive quantities of literature? For want of realities, there is an overproduction of symbols;
which is, moreover, understandable since normal levels of production
amongst the colonized would not compensate for their overall lack of
productivity. Overproduce or perish. Survive or disappear. Surprise or
possess nothing. These are matters of life and death for the dominated.

Yes, to be dominated is to live a novel written in advance, to conform unconsciously to patterns of behaviour which are sufficiently ambiguous for their meaning to escape those who are caught up in them.
For example, while the dominated are demanding their rights, they are
not aware of the degree of complementarity that exists between master
and petitioner, or of the good will with which the former agrees to
respond, conceding just enough to allow the petitioner to think from
time to time that he has won the game. And everything falls invisibly

back into place. . . . To refuse this coherence is to opt, wholeheartedly and irrevocably, for incoherence. To choose revolution is to step outside the dialogue which binds dominator and dominated; to be exact, it is to ramble. The terrorist speaks alone. Like Hamlet, the sweet prince of the rotten kingdom, imagining Gertrude's lover behind every arras, the revolutionary chooses to be thought mad. The revolutionary breaks with the coherence of domination, rashly launching into a monologue interrupted at every word, finding inspiration in the hesitant pauses which mark the distance separating him from the dominant mode of thought. Hesitation gives birth to monologue; in the theatre, the only characters who are given monologues are those who hesitate indefinitely, who are grappling with the distorting isolation of the revolutionary or the madman. Only in incoherence are true monologues possible. The incoherence I am talking about here is one of the modalities of revolution, just as monologue is its unmistakable sign.

Incoherence corresponds, in Hamlet's case at least, to being irrevocably out of phase with the old coherence. Hamlet suddenly falls apart. And since, from that moment on, he acts outside any laws of coherence, he stops being human "in the full sense of the word," as the psychoanalyst André Lussier might say. I know that Freud was aware of being Jewish and that, through his transcending desire for coherence, he overcame this detail, as one rises above one's myopia, to rid himself of all Jewishness and see the world in a larger, more Austrian perspective. The French Canadian who cannot go on alone tries to broaden his horizons and lose himself in a non-group whose dominating position escapes his attention and which generously provides him with a coherent non-identity. In a neo-colonial situation, literary activity expresses an attitude of acceptance. Furthermore, the rites of literary creation are generally recognized as having a therapeutic effect; after a night of endless ecstasy, the dancer does not have the energy to respond to the colonial sphynx. The ritual of the dance of words on the horizon reconciles man to his unreality, while at the same time exhausting him. In our shattered country, I refuse the solace that I have sought for too long a time in the stammering ceremony of writing. Now the disintegration has begun, I feel a serene desire to participate in the putrefaction of our crumbling society; I have an unholy appetite for the body and blood (both foreign) mouldering away during the multibilingual sessions of a twenty-second royal commission, nailing me contagiously to the cross.

One day—who knows?—it may be given to us to write sanely; to write and for it to be something other than an exorcism, something other than a divisive distraction. If, dear reader, at the end of my Cartesian flight you have the impression that I am preaching compulsory political commitment for writers, then that is sufficient reason for me to keep you back after class. Compulsory military service is odious and, what is more, paves the way for defeat. The same is true of compulsory intellectual service for those citizens of eighteen and over who are capable of living a great love affair on a typewriter keyboard. No writer is required to toe the literary line laid down according to the options of a particular political system, any more than he is committed by his wordmongering to take a vow of historical chastity and renounce all but the production of a posthumous and autarkical work of art.

Jean Simard defines the literary endeavour as "the most exciting of all adventures—that of our inner world. From book to book the writer pursues a never-ending self-examination. It is a commitment of the entire self in the relentless search of each individual for his own truth" (*Le Devoir*, Saturday, 7 December 1963, p. 11). What better expression of the inalienable right of writers to spend their evenings at home! The inner world represents the cage which one leaves only to go to the Dominican bookstore (closed on Sundays) to stock up on the books written by other writers who have invested in their own little microcosm. For me, a blasphemer, the term "inner adventure" evokes the clammy exchanges of a disarmament conference between the emissaries of countries ready to go to war. Or rather, the inner adventure of the writer is the migration of the living yolk inside the hermetically sealed shell of the egg. A viscous adventure: a fight to the finish between the abortable yolk and its albuminous sphincter. Whatever the demonstrated index of euphemization of the endeavours of those writers who think they are sailing on the high seas when they are cruising in their little duckponds, they cannot with impunity refuse the implications of their constitutionally lacklustre status as inventors of variants in their vacillating country, the collective site of bouts of fever and senile dementia. The "inner" adventure of French Canada changes even those who have chosen to specialize in their literary micro-adventures.

The modified statutes of Elizabeth II, Queen of Canada and (Northern!) Ireland, the matriloquacious Queen of every province and of unilingual St. Jérôme and of Quebec at Cap de la Madeleine, do not stipulate that it is forbidden to play Mozart's "Turkish March," standing stock-still in the middle of a political crisis. The revised or (more evocatively) exploded statutes of Lord Snowdon's sister-in-law contain no provision for the punishment of those who cultivate the flowers of style while the national heartbeat portends upheaval, if not the bleeding to death of our political system. Such queenly courtesy, this civilly coded silence on the subject of the inner world of crypto-Gaelic writers in times of trouble. What is not specifically forbidden according to the letter of the law is implicitly authorized or legitimate. Thus there is nothing to stop one from word-mongering with the help of dictionary-authenticated phenomena. Writers can rest easy should their libido call for a little knitting. And it goes without saying that knitting in no way excludes ceramics, for there is no principle of segregation which would allow those who penelope on their Smith-Coronas to think themselves superior to those with a marked preference for the kiln. In all cases of inner adventure, recorded daily like the minutes of a meeting, everything is permitted; free rein is given to the talents of every individual. And there is no doubt that the "inner adventure" evoked by the recently fêted Jean Simard[3] requires a certain amount of perseverance and courage, for the simple reason that it has no strong motivation and that it is possible to continue with the higher work only by sanctifying writing as a duty.

The writer does not choose his native land, but the "inner adventurer" is wrong to live there as though he were living in another country, in an exhausting act of transference onto a super-country and in a continual state of denaturalization. Every word written by an absentee writer carries a coefficient "n" of intense inanity. This coefficient could also be indexed to allow his work to be quoted (in terms of market value and redemption value) on a daily basis like an ordinary share. One does not choose one's native land; still, it is better to put down roots and take nourishment, symbiotically, from this cold earth we have trodden since childhood. It is better, for the writer who turns to inner adventures as others do to styrofoam insulation (rather than the cork lining which protected Proust to the end), it is better for him to live in his country than to transport himself to an artistic and grammatical non-country where every foreigner enjoys literary immunity. The non-country does not nourish its man. The mental Switzerland of the 1917 vintage Byelorussians promotes the pursuit of inner adventures, so long as they are regulated by the canons of disarmament. But even if the writer can venture there as he likes, with breakfast in bed and the hotel guest's impeccable xenophobia, this miniature inner Switzerland is nothing but a coffin decorated like the Place des Arts. All in all, it is preferable to hate one's country than to detach oneself from it while all the time hoping to give expression to it. How does one express deficiency? That is the real problem. It seems to me that the adulterous love of one's country is still more beautiful than abstinence in the name of what Jean Simard calls a "commitment to the Work itself and to the cultivation of one's own being for the sake of the work" (*Le Devoir*, Saturday, 26 October 1963).

There is an implacable correlation between an individual's self-awareness and the country of his birth. I no longer believe in an authorial immunity which exempts the writer—committed exclusively to his work—from living in his country. It is sterile to use one's own land only in slices of life which, through their anthological status, clearly establish the writer's lack of roots. In this way, the writer ends up conferring special status on his "inner" experience, thereby eviscerating it in advance when he is not soaking himself in a jar of formaldehyde like some pathetic specimen, the latest dodo threatened, like us, with extinction. In a country in a state of ontological gestation, the writer's calling cannot remain unchanged; nor can it be pursued, even with courage, according to the futile categories of the sublime and the important. The inner adventure that so many writers dream of living despite the manic depression which characterizes the life of our group is a prefabricated work, portable like a typewriter, finished before it is started, an enclosure to be interred in the archives. Yet many are the writers who go on climbing, one word at a time, the Laurentian Calvary of the Work—with a capital "W" for Whitewash. But the numbers do nothing to change their splendid aberration. Now that everything around him is infected with the gangrene of uncertainty, the writer has less reason than ever to claim episcopal status or an exemption from reality or a dispensation from pain. Syntax, form, the meaning of words—all are subject to explosion. In a country which is blacking out, the writer who attempts to breathe life into what is killing him will not write a Stendhalian tale of French-Canadian *carbonari*, but a work as uncertain and formally unwholesome as the one taking place in him and in his country. The problem is not one of being a member of the PSQ or the RIN or the PRQ,[4] or of stuffing envelopes in a typically disorganized party office. The problem for the writer is to live in his country, to die and be resurrected with it. The revolution operating mysteriously in each and every one of us is skewing the old French language, exploding its inherited structures which, through the strict adherence of those who respected them, exercised a unilateral hegemony over the collective mind. The old idea of the work, predictable, serene and a model of stability, keeps slipping into unconsciousness, a victim of those same blackouts that my country has known in the past and has come to fear, so many winters which may or may not be followed by springs.

During this period of troubles, how could the writer finish his sentence the way he had planned? Everything is changing and threatening to change; how can anyone who chooses to write persist with an unchanging ideal of the literary work as coming first? Such an attitude can lead only to the production of historical monuments. There is nothing transcendent about the work of literature or about our collective adventure. To want not to bear witness or to bear witness leaving out segments of our life and our obsession is to bear witness anyway. It is a waste of time to write novels unsullied by the intolerable realities of our collective daily life, in an antiseptic French untouched by the spasms which shake the ground we walk on. My passport bears the words "Occupation: writer." Even if I deny the writer in me, what use is it to fill out forms declaring that I am no longer a writer, at least not the writer I wanted to be when I filled out the application for a passport on 23 September 1958? My passport has already expired. But then, I will never leave my native land again. I want to stay here. I live in my country.

["Profession: écrivain." *Parti pris* I, no. 4 (January 1964): 23–31.]

Editor's Notes

1. Founded in October 1963, *Parti pris* was a radical nationalist journal of politics and culture, drawing for its ideological positions on Marxism, Sartrean existentialism and socialist decolonization.
2. Paul Comtois was appointed lieutenant governor of Quebec in October 1961.
3. Jean Simard was the 1963 winner of the Prix Duvernay, a literary prize established in 1944 by the Catholic-nationalist St. Jean-Baptiste Society.
4. Respectively: the Parti Socialiste du Québec, the Rassemblement pour l'Indépendance Nationale and the Parti Républicain du Québec. For further details, see the notes to "The Politics of Existence," pp. 17–18.

The Mystic Body

There is good reason to believe that metaphors are really apocryphal confessions bearing a large freight of unconscious material. The significance of apparently meaningless details was demonstrated long ago. One might say that there are not many people who can pride themselves on saying only what they mean in order to flaunt their immaculate inanity. I would not have given a second thought to some of the interpretations which come to mind concerning federal-provincial terminology, had I not come across unsought for parallels in the pronouncements of our public figures. Generally speaking, the perception of Confederation in terms of the coexistence of two nations seems to conjure up the image either of a sexual relationship pushed to disgusting extremes or of a Christian marriage, failed but indissoluble, between a Pisces and an Aries. Confederation can thus be understood rhetorically according to the various forms of the "bonds" of love.

59

Here are a few working hypotheses which I offer in the hope that they may lay to rest the thematics of the unmade bed.

Theme of the Shotgun Wedding

"The fact that Confederation is a marriage of convenience is," according to Mr. Lamontagne, "a mixed blessing. While it is true that it is weakened by the absence of love, it is strengthened by the fact that it is dictated by our economic interest... " ("We shall be the fathers of a new Confederation," in *La Presse*).[1]

"Lesage urges English Canadians to espouse the constitutional demands of their francophone fellow-citizens" (front page headline in *Le Devoir*, 11 July 1963).

Lamontagne's allusion to the "economic interest" which constitutes the strength of the marriage and Jean Lesage's indecent propositioning of English Canadians indicate quite clearly that, according to the logic peculiar to this sexualization of Confederation, it is Quebec which is cast in the role of the woman. This marriage of convenience brings no love, but the wife is none the less a consenting prisoner of the marriage, since she enjoys no economic power which, as we know, is a typically male prerogative, an extension of virility measured in money.

Theme of the Frigid Woman

"Sexual feeling may be entirely absent. The woman may miss both the forepleasure and the orgasm. . . . The women admit that they are glowing with yearnings, that they crave the orgasm, but complain that they are unable to attain it."[2]

"Separatism has acted for some years now as a stimulant. . . . Those who embrace it assume an attitude of expectation. They may work very hard to have the grace of independence formally bestowed upon them. The chief obstacles are to be found in ourselves, in our laziness and our apathy, in the mediocrity of our desires, in our fickleness... " (André Laurendeau, "Yesterday's stimulant, tomorrow's pretext for escape?" in *Le Devoir*, Wednesday, 26 June 1963).[3]

What could be more "feminine" than this "attitude of expectation" that Laurendeau projects onto the separatist faction? And what could be more frigid, in thought if not in flesh, than placing such an inflated value on stimulants and resigning oneself before the fact to the mediocrity of one's desires? Here the *anaesthesia sexualis feminarum* goes hand in hand with a moral code of marriage which attributes aphrodisiac properties to the FLQ[4] and separatism, both of which are forbidden modes of behaviour. Here is a variation on this idea by the same author: "Two external stimulants have played a part. Firstly separatism, which has gone on growing, especially in intellectual circles, and which has even led to violence (and we still don't know what shape separatism will be in when it emerges from its misadventure with the FLQ). Hitherto, it has served as a goad. The political power of the separatist groups is clearly very slight. But they keep on reasserting the absolute goal of independence, broadcasting their message in an ever widening arc, though the masses have not (at least for the time being) been reached" (*Le Devoir*, 22 June 1963).

The explicitly tactile terms used in this article to refer to the separatist stimulant can only come from the mind of a spouse who is doubly frustrated because she is not only faithful but frozen. But the anaesthetization of the erogenous zones does not prevent the mind from framing, though not without bitterness, the marital problem.

"On this new level," writes Father Arès, "the most important question is whether or not Canadians—all Canadians—want there to be a Canada. This question has to be answered, and as soon as possible, not only with vague words but with actions. Nowadays, all the indications are that Canada is founded uniquely on the Anglo-French union. There is no alternative: Canada will be Anglo-French or will not exist at all" (Richard Arès, "If the majority does not agree... ," in *La Presse*, May 1963).[5]

Theme of Divorce Italian-style

"If husband and wife cannot learn to sleep together, then they should certainly have separate beds. It is a matter of urgent concern, for you as for us, that we all be aware of the fact that we do not sleep well in a bed in which *you* lie obliviously snoring" (René Lévesque, in *La Presse*, May 1963).[6]

Theme of Mortal Insults

Irreparable by definition, insults involve excesses which we will be forgiven for quoting: "If Quebec separates, it will become a kind of banana republic" (Murray Ballantyne, in *La Presse*, 17 June 1963). The somewhat malevolent use of the metaphorical banana marks a stylistic shift from the dialogue of the deaf carried on between spouses legally linked in a manic embrace to the dialogue of a musical comedy in the worst possible taste. Moreover, Murray Ballantyne lives up to his role of perfect ingrate, adding in frustration: "Life would be so much simpler if we were to abandon the Canadian experiment. . . . " He even goes so far as to make indelicate allusions to the neighbour he would have preferred if truth were known: "It would be to our advantage to cast in our lot with the United States. . . . " The wife who suddenly finds herself held up to ridicule screams blue murder: "Our autonomy is being raped by Ottawa—Lesage" (*La Presse*, 26 June 1963). This charge of rape throws the accused off balance; he backs off and announces off the record that "a first joint venture has been terminated," claiming, by this clever move, the right to sum up the situation in a few words—at the expense, of course, of the paranoid wife. "The Québécois think that their province is being stifled by English Canada," says George Ferguson before a gathering in Edmonton, apparently unembarrassed by this display of marital discord: "Mr. Ferguson added that there was no love lost between French Canada and English Canada" (*La Presse*, December 1963). And then, carried away by an excess of enthusiasm, someone goes too far: "A single language, English, is all that is needed to unite Canada," declares a certain Ralph Cowan. Even if she is hurt and cannot hold back the tears, the spouse has no qualms about spelling out the bottom line of this experiment in living together: "The federal balance sheet is negative. In the red in every respect. Confederation is sick. Its illness goes beyond the persons of Mr. Pearson or Mr. Lamontagne and their friends. . . " (Gérard Pelletier— of all people!— in his *La Presse*, December 1963).[7]

But just because a marriage is failing on all counts, it does not follow that it is time to start afresh. Not when one has been accustomed from birth to being thankful for small mercies.

"Do French Canadians have a marked tendency to states of depression? If the study carried out by professors at the University of Montreal is to be believed, it would seem that the answer has to be yes. In her paper given at the meeting of ACFAS, Mme Roussin advanced the following hypothesis based on a study of the files of two psychiatric hospitals, one French and one English: in comparison with English Canadians, French Canadians are much more prone to depressive behaviour" (from a paper presented at ACFAS—Association canadienne-française pour l'avancement des sciences—in 1963).

It is not unusual to see these states of depression degenerate into a noticeable regression to the oral stage: "You cannot try to build a country around a language!" (Reverend Father Benoît Lacroix, in *La Presse*, June 1963). This disheartening pronouncement seems typical of the etiology of the spouse in a state of oral regression—a dangerous descent into a not-too-distant national past when the language expressed, through verbigeration and bouts of echolalia, the national will to live of the mentally deficient wife.

Theme of the Lonelyhearts Column

Then along comes the friend of the couple with his pat prognosis to straighten everything out: "Premier Robichaud[8] predicts the death of separatism. . . . It is a movement which turns up every now and then, but which is destined to disappear; in any case, there is nothing for us to worry about. . . " (*La Presse*, 1 November 1963). But the kind words of the friend do not settle much at all. Then there is nothing for it but to make for the confessional and confess everything, even if it hurts, to Doctor Michael Oliver,[9] whose fame rests on his ability to discourage his patients by means of a tried and tested homeopathic technique of public healing. To hear him, you would think that he was in pain, and there are those who say that ontologically his sympathies lie with those who have been flayed alive: "The schisms which have appeared hitherto in the associations trying to build a bridge between the two solitudes can now bring those agencies which have remained intact (and there are a lot of them) to a better understanding of the kind of internal reorganization required to ensure their stability. But such a happy outcome can only be achieved by containing on all fronts the tendency to dissolution."

And then, we have to admit that the Faust from McGill is blessed with an unusual degree of psychological acumen, which makes him a serious rival for Father Desmarais[10]: "One can scarcely take the liberty of ridiculing the pessimists who predict that the breakup of the parts is simply a prelude to that of the whole." Michael Oliver, our pan-Canadian director of conscience, demystifies with gentlemanly lucidity an old myth of which I for one was unaware: "Too often," he writes in *La Presse* of 5 November 1963, "have we taken as model for our Anglo-French association a team of ill-matched horses wearing enormous blinkers." By so lucidly rejecting the solution of the two horses, the professor furthers the concept of two nations and spares us the necessity of thinking of Confederation as a "team" and of our common problems as a kind of vulgar crupper.

Theme of the Mother-in-law

But when all is said and done... "Peter Desbarats is of the opinion that the first outburst of separatism has given way to a period of calm.... Peter Desbarats is of the opinion that the population of Quebec has rallied over the last few months to the point of view of those who want to give the Anglo-Saxon element in Canada another chance.... It would seem that Quebec has consciously entered a period of constructive effort... " (*La Presse*, 7 November 1963).

Theme of Reconciliation

"We can never be more faithful to our origins than by remaining within Confederation" (Jean Lesage, in *La Presse*, 12 October 1963). "If Quebec is to play a healthy part in a real Confederation, then we must have a completely positive outlook. We must beware the slippery slope of demands and the trap of too much talk... " (René Lévesque, in *Le Devoir*, 5 July 1963).

Of course, one has to come to some agreement with a partner and, as Jean-Luc Pépin[11] tells us, in marriage as in anything else one has to be realistic: "It's like love; you ask for more to be sure of having at least half" (*Le Devoir*, 3 December 1963). With these words, Mr. Pépin takes us back to the marital reality of Confederation which naturally, as one might expect, will have its petty quarrels—mere trifles, of course. There is no cause for alarm then, since even nations have their menstrual cycles and their mood swings according to the laws of nature. A sedative will suffice to bring Quebec's behaviour under control during these lunar periods.

Theme of Federal Transcendence

Pearson: "I do not want to witness the liquidation of Canada" (eight-column headline in *Le Devoir*, 13 November 1963). If we accept such terms as "liquidation" which, I admit, enjoy a high index of pan-Canadian sexualization, we can see in Pearson's themes an apocalyptic obsession which is quite touching. Pearson's level is that of the mystic body of federalism, and his vocabulary, like that of the Apostle of Patmos, reveals his eschatological version of the Holy Land of Canada, which is inevitably the object of the shameful, earthly desires of Pearson's vicars. Fortunately for the perfect anchorite Pearson, a faithful disciple is dedicated to spreading the confederate gospel amongst us heathens and this valiant apostle has consented to find words in our language to express the sibylline oracles of his master.

Even if this free and sometimes even simultaneous translation is not as holy as the gospel according to the Nobel Peace Prize,[12] it is no less commendable since it shows the same tautological intensity and, what is more, has popular appeal. As the fragments of this vulgate have not been scientifically collected in a definitive album, let me quote here a single line which gives a fair idea of the evangelical range of the preaching of Mr. Lamontagne (for whom beatification proceedings are to begin shortly). On October 15, 1963—it was a dismal Tuesday as I recall —I read the following headline in the evening paper : "There will still be a Confederation in 1967—Maurice Lamontagne." Poor devil...

["Le corps mystique." *Parti pris* I, no. 5 (February 1964): 30–36.]

Editor's Notes

1. Maurice Lamontagne was a member of the Pearson cabinet from 1963 to 1965.
2. Wilhelm Stekel, *Frigidity in Woman in Relation to her Love Life*, authorized English version by James S. Van Teslaar (New York: Washington Square Press, 1967, c1926), p. 102.

3. André Laurendeau was co-chairman of the Royal Commission on Bilingualism and Biculturalism (1963–1964) and editor-in-chief of *Le Devoir*.

4. It was in 1963 that the first bombing campaigns were mounted by the FLQ (Front de libération du Québec).

5. The editor of the journal *Relations*, Father Richard Arès had written extensively on Confederation and on constitutional questions. In December 1962 he published *Du Rôle de l'état dans un Québec fort* and, in June 1963, *Justice et équité pour la communauté canadienne-française*, both pamphlets in the collection "Questions actuelles."

6. From 1961 to 1965, René Lévesque was minister of Natural Resources in Jean Lesage's Liberal government.

7. Editor-in-chief of the Montreal daily *La Presse* from June 1961 to March 1965, Gérard Pelletier would be elected as a federal Liberal M.P. in 1965 along with the other two "wise men," Pierre Elliott Trudeau and Jean Marchand.

8. Louis-J. Robichaud was the first Acadian to be elected premier of New Brunswick.

9. Professor of Political Science at McGill and head of the Research Bureau of the Royal Commission on Bilingualism and Biculturalism, Michael Oliver was co-editor with Frank Scott of *Quebec States her Case* (1964).

10. The Dominican Father Marcel-Marie Desmarais was a radio and television personality and the author of a number of best-selling books on religion and popular psychology.

11. A professor, journalist and member of the federal Liberal party, Jean-Luc Pépin was elected for the first time in April 1963.

12. Lester Pearson, prime minister of Canada from 1963 to 1968, had won the Nobel Peace Prize in 1957.

The Art of Defeat: A Matter of Style

Name: Indignity; first name: Humiliation; status: Revolt...
Aimé Césaire

The rebellion of 1837–1838, a veritable anthology of agonizing mistakes, blunders and botched attempts, was fought and lived by the *Patriotes* like a lost cause. The theories of Clausewitz and Moltke were forever laid to rest by the heroic exploits of our precious rebellion, at least in the sense that the coefficient of imponderability that is present in any military encounter was in this instance reduced to zero. Everything *was* foreseeable—everything! And everything was foreseen; nothing was left to chance (because you never know—chance might just lead you to victory!). The rebellion of 1837–1838 is incontrovertible evidence that French Canadians are capable of anything, even of conspiring in their own defeat.

You will object that the *Patriotes'* arsenal was not sufficiently well-stocked for them to take on Colborne's troops;[1] not enough double-barrelled rifles or enough gunpowder, not enough money stolen from industry to buy Winchesters in the Montreal stores, and so on and so forth. I have heard them all before, these objective explanations for the *Patriotes'* defeat: not enough guns, or cartridges, or cannon, or career officers. Yes, yes, I know—they make a fine excuse which Engels spelled out for us: "Violence is not simply a matter of will; if it is to become a reality, it requires very specific conditions and, in particular, the right instruments, the more perfect of which will triumph over the less perfect; in short, violence depends for its success on arms production, which in turn depends on production in general; therefore… " According to the compelling logic of Engels's argument, the *Patriotes'* only mistake was not to have built, on the banks of the Richelieu, a large munitions factory, itself a logical component of a vast industrial complex comprising a foundry (for the cannon), a cartridge plant, and a large mill for the mass production of dress uniforms and battle fatigues for the officers and men of the army of Lower Canada. Right. So much for logic—which I humbly salute but fail to understand. For it so happens that I have also heard about some Spanish peasants who, less educated and not as well armed as the *Patriotes*, managed to turn back Napoleon's Grand Army, using tactics that have since come to be known as guerilla warfare. That was in 1810. "Yet," comments Frantz Fanon, "the French army made the whole of Europe tremble by its weapons of war, by the bravery of its soldiers and by the military genius of its leaders. Face to face with the enormous potentials of the Napoleonic troops, the Spaniards, inspired by an unshakeable national ardour, rediscovered the famous methods of guerilla warfare which, twenty-five years before, the American militia had tried out on the English forces."[2] I find this last remark particularly appealing. According to Fanon, the Americans (in our own backyard) used guerilla warfare in 1776, before the term was ever invented, against the loyal troops of George III; what is more, these troops were in every respect similar to those patrolling the Richelieu valley in 1837. The *Patriotes* did not know the word "guerilla," but they certainly were fans, so to speak, of the American Revolution, boosting their morale with tales from this war of independence in which the Davids finally triumphed over the Goliaths.[3]

We now know that the distribution of arms and munitions is not a reliable guide to the outcome of revolutionary wars. I would even go so far as to say that one of the characteristic features of revolutionary wars is precisely this unequal distribution of arms and resources, an inequality which is reversed in the course of the struggle by the determination of an entire population to seize its independence. Which is not to say that the choice of arms is unimportant. Far from it! As the hostilities progress, it is essential to take over the enemy's arms—but never his strategy!

In October 1837, the *Patriotes* were not ready for war, in that they lacked the necessary military hardware. On the other hand, they did have leaders, generals, intelligent clear-headed men commanding them; and they had the people on their side and the greatest cause in the world to defend—freedom! Moreover, the *Patriotes* knew the terrain and the hinterland, knew where to camp and where to find shelter in the woods. Then at St. Denis, all hell broke loose and the *Patriotes*, bewildered by the flight of Papineau, armed with whatever they could lay their hands on (and let us not forget that this was their first taste of battle, so they had every excuse for losing their heads), opened the hostilities with a decisive victory over the English troops under Gore,[4] himself an experienced and well-respected soldier. A morale-raising victory, and rightly so; the revolution needed the inspiring example of this success in order to mobilize both troops and opinion.

But already at St. Denis, something strange happened: they were afraid, in the words of Lionel Groulx, "to press home their advantage and give chase to Gore's companies, which were fleeing before them in total disarray."[5] The first sign of weakness—a strange and mysterious collective *lapsus* coming from men who had given a spectacular display of cool-headed teamwork. It was like being at a performance of a classical tragedy during which the chorus, all at once and in the most unlikely unanimity, forgets its lines. A deathly silence ensues. What exactly is going on? Not another word from any mouth; the tragedy is interrupted so suddenly that the audience is distinctly ill at ease. The chorus has lost its voice. How can so many men forget their lines at the same time? Unless... yes; unless they haven't forgotten their lines at all? The chorus cannot go on because the other actors have not said the words they were supposed to say—a hypothesis which provides an explanation for what is happening on stage. The chorus, dumbstruck, cannot say its lines if what has just happened on stage was not in the script; the *Patriotes* did not forget their lines at St. Denis, but were thrown by an event which was not part of the play: their own victory!

They had been convinced that theirs would be a glorious death under the fire of real soldiers; then, when they found themselves carrying the day, they did not know what to do next; surprised by an unlikely turn of events, paralyzed by a totally unforeseen victory, they were struck dumb, terrified because now they would have to go on with the war. Thus far, they had prepared themselves to die with honour, but there they were, still alive and having to make fresh plans, having to marshal their forces like a real army since, all unwittingly, they had been recast as victors. The victorious company of St. Denis did not press home its advantage because, like the Light Brigade before its famous charge, the *Patriotes* had prepared, with a light heart, only for their own death and destruction. It had certainly never occurred to them—valiant company that they were—that they were embarking on a war and that, consequently, they would have to go on with the show. Conditioned to defeat as others are to suicide, because it is the honourable thing to do, the *Patriotes* suddenly found themselves having to survive without honour, without style, without even the hope of one day having done with it all. That sudden moment of comprehension must have been a terrible one indeed, and it is understandable, to me, that they should have faltered, as though thunderstruck by the prospect of a future quite unlike anything they had foreseen.

Between November 23 and November 25 what happened?

A period of inactivity. Then the battle of St. Charles: the heroes of St. Denis, disoriented, slip silently and shamefacedly into a posture of submission. The English, as always, make war in the same way that they play cricket. Like good colonials, the *Patriotes* stick to the rules of the game and behave, with a politeness born of despair, like gentlemen. No low blows, no French frenzy; no tricks (or none worth writing home about), nothing untoward in their table manners. One eats like one's host. One fights like him, too; and, when it comes to making war against the English, we do exactly what we were taught to do, under their orders, against the Americans in 1812. As in any violent sport, there are risks and the occasional accident; well, those are the rules of the game and we won't let it be said that we are bad sports. Phlegmatic but unimaginative, we play the game with quiet despair; we get murdered, but the umpire is always right; we lose, but there is nothing surprising in that. It was in the cards; we almost wanted to lose. And then, when it is all over, we go on fraternizing with the conqueror, who himself is obliged to be a good sport since we are such good losers.

"Ill-protected in makeshift camps, they stayed put," writes Lionel Groulx,[6] "waiting awkwardly for the enemy to arrive, when they could have engaged him in irregular warfare, harrassing him on the roads." What pains me about this rebellion is precisely the passivity of the loser—the noble and desperate passivity of someone who will never be surprised to lose, but who will be all at sea should he happen to win. What pains me even more is that their carefully botched adventure perpetuates, from generation to generation, the image of a conquered hero. Some countries remember an unknown soldier, but we have no choice: the soldier we commemorate is famous in defeat, a soldier whose incredible sadness goes on working within us like a force of inertia. It is no small matter, at that point, to embark on a national revolution which our forebears did such a perfect job of bungling. They even managed to bungle it with exemplary courage. The *Patriotes* took to despair with a perverse persistence; they went to war but could never be accused of wanting to win at all costs. That probably explains why they forgot their lines after the victory at St. Denis and the suicidal style of their tactics. Their rebellion, so tragic in its disorder, resembles the poetic project of a man who has grown indifferent to the forms of his failure. Is it possible to commit so many errors of basic strategy when one is Wolfred Nelson, Chénier or J.-J. Girouard?[7] No. Their errors go beyond the very concept of error, and the confusion in which they worked is radically different from any other kind of confusion; in fact, their failure—and I am almost afraid to say this—looks like a long-premeditated one, a Gothic masterpiece of madness. These men, whom I cannot help but like even if it causes me pain, tried to put an end to the state of humiliation in which we still live today. The whole of Lower Canada was destroyed in the unbearable spectacle of its own defeat. Our *Patriotes* were men, if only because they were unwavering in their being-for-defeat.

The *Patriotes* did not fail for want of talent, nor for lack of military science, nor even because they were short of money; they took up arms joyfully and with the certainty of putting an end to a long drawn out agony.

According to Mao Tse-Tung, it is essential to win the first battle: "Its success or failure has a tremendous effect upon the whole situation, and affects even the final engagement."[8] And to think that the *Patriotes* won their first battle! To think that, in so doing, they obeyed one of the laws of revolutionary warfare, an instinctive and unwritten law, poetically expressed more than a century later in the laconic style of Mao Tse-Tung. All things considered, the war of national liberation got off to a perfect and explosive start with that first battle at St. Denis. What a dazzling debut for a rag-bag army of *Patriotes* and what a way to open! The first act of the rebellion was a complete success, a revolutionary triumph which came close to perfection. The *Patriotes'* victory at St. Denis unfolded like a triumphal prelude to the war of independence of Lower Canada. It is impossible for an armed revolution to start more auspiciously. But what then? "When Marx said that once an armed uprising is started there must not be a moment's pause in the attack, he meant that the masses, having taken the enemy by surprise in an uprising, must not allow the reactionary ruling classes any chance to retain or recover their political power, but must seize this moment to spring a surprise attack on the nation's reactionary ruling forces, and that they must never feel satisfied with the victories they have won, underrate the enemy, relent in their attacks on the enemy, or hesitate to go forward so as to miss the chance of annihilating the enemy and court failure for the revolution."[9] Court failure for the revolution, says Mao Tse-Tung who, when he wrote those lines, was probably not thinking of the strange paralysis which afflicted the victors of St. Denis or of that sudden blackout which opened up an abyss of hesitation between the first battle of 1837 and all the defeats that followed. St. Denis was the start of a great adventure which, without the total commitment it demanded, was doomed from the outset to end in disaster.

I should like, in conclusion, to make clear that there was a world of difference between the style of the rebellion of 1837 and that of the invasion of 1838. The battles of 1838 were not in the same vein as those of 1837. The revolutionary action of 1838 was more like the beginning of a genuine war of national liberation; this time the *Patriotes* used quite different methods and tactics from those employed by Wolfred Nelson and Chénier. The differences were considerable and self-evident. In the first place, the *Patriotes* sought help from outside the country in an attempt to give their revolution something of an international dimension. Moreover, they invented an across the board strategy specifically designed to defeat their enemy, involving secret recruiting and infiltration through the *Frères Chasseurs*,[10] a programme of officer training (Hindenlang, Touvrey and two Polish officers were recruited that way[11]) and "revolutionary" financing through thefts from the factories and "bonds" issued on the future Republic of Lower Canada. The *Patriotes* of 1838 intended to stay on the offensive and decided to launch a surprise attack at several points at once to throw the regular troops off balance (cf. "The Plot of November 3" in this issue of *Liberté*, p. 191). And so, after the catastrophic events of 1837 culminating in the disaster of St. Eustache, those who regrouped in the United States under the leadership of Robert Nelson *wanted* to succeed and prepared for victory using tricks, ploys, spies, primitive forms of "terrorism" and the whole gamut of offensive strategies used in revolutionary warfare. From which we can conclude that Robert Nelson and Chevalier de Lorimier,[12] the dominant figures in the 1838 invasion, were true *Patriotes* whose coefficient of passivity tended to zero. They were not *Patriotes* driven to take up arms by the arrogant and vexatious decrees of some governor; they were not rebels against their own better judgment. No, they chose the path of revolutionary war as a way of liberating their country and establishing once and for all the Republic of Lower Canada. That their armed struggle was clearly political is shown by the formation of a provisional government under the presidency of Robert Nelson and the declaration of independence of the Republic of Lower Canada.[13]

While Nelson's troops were being transformed into a real army of guerilla fighters, Colborne's men stepped up their recruiting and their manoeuvres and prepared to do battle themselves. The forces of repression, mobilized by the impact of the 1837 rebellion, had time to get themselves organized and make provision for a more adequate counter-offensive than in 1837.

The mistake made by the *Patriotes* of 1838 cannot be explained in terms of a failure of their will to win or by the use of outmoded tactics; their mistake was to underestimate the enemy and to make the implicit assumption that it would be the same kind of enemy as in 1837. Whereas, in fact, the regular forces had much greater mobility in 1838 and their ability to counter-attack was at once more rapid and more devastating. Colborne's secret preparations were, moreover, clearly effective, since he was informed by his spies well in advance of the plot of November 3 and was already, by that date, on a real war footing. The surprise effect that the *Patriotes* had counted on was completely lost. Now, when one is counting above all on surprise (and not on numbers or on force of arms) to throw the enemy off stride, and the enemy knows about everything and prepares accordingly, one is lucky to escape with anything less than total annihilation. The defeat of 1838 took only a week, whereas in 1837 the battles had raged for about a month. Such a lightning defeat is attributable to the state of readiness of Colborne's troops rather than to any lack of readiness on the part of the *Patriotes* of the "invasion." The legacy of 1837 was precisely this mobilization of the forces of reaction, resulting in a greatly accentuated disparity in strength between the *Patriotes* of 1838 and the troops awaiting them at the border. The *Patriotes*, after the dismal sequence of events of 1837, had changed completely; but the situation had changed too. Even Colborne's troops had learned something from the lesson of 1837, and an enemy forewarned is an enemy forearmed.

On the eve of his execution, Chevalier de Lorimier wrote to his children that their father's crime was to have failed. What clarity of mind compared with the vacillations of a Papineau, his sudden exile on the eve of battle and the sad self-vindication written from Paris! Chevalier de Lorimier was not a part-time *Patriote*; he knew what he was doing and why he was doing it. He knew, too, that when you embark on a war of national liberation, you have to succeed or end up on the gallows. George Washington, commanding the American revolutionaries in 1776, had said: "If I am not hanged, I will be President." Washington became President; de Lorimier was hanged. That is the logic of revolution: "succeed or die."

["L'art de la défaite: considérations stylistiques."
Liberté VII, no. 1–2 (January-April 1965): 33–41.]

Notes

Most of the notes to this essay are Aquin's own. Where I have made significant changes or additions, other than supplying references to English translations of works cited wherever possible, this is indicated in parentheses after the note. (*Ed.*)

1. Sir John Colborne, a seasoned soldier and former lieutenant governor, was commander of the military forces in Canada during the rebellions of 1837–1838. (*Ed.*)
2. Frantz Fanon, *The Wretched of the Earth*, trans. Constance Farrington (New York: Grove Press, 1963), p. 51.
3. "The best political doctrines of modern times are, to my mind, set out in condensed form and entrusted to the love of the peoples for their regeneration in a few lines of

the Declaration of Independence of 1776 and the Declaration of the Rights of Man of 1789. . . . " Louis-Joseph Papineau, quoted by Fernand Ouellet in the *Cahiers de l'Institut d'Histoire de l'Université Laval*, no. 1.

4. Colonel Sir Charles Gore was Colborne's Quartermaster General. (*Ed.*)

5. Lionel Groulx, *Histoire du Canada français*, fourth edition (Montreal & Paris: Fides, 1962), vol. II, pp. 163–64.

6. Ibid., p. 163. The "irregular warfare" referred to by Groulx was suited in several respects to the circumstances of 1837. Thus, when the rebel troops are scattered, when the number of soldiers does not command victory, "then it is precisely because of their numerical weakness that the partisan units can operate behind enemy lines, appearing and disappearing as if by magic. The very inferiority of the partisan units can allow them to take the initiative. Such freedom of movement is denied the regular troops, which are lacking in flexibility. In partisan warfare, the question of the initiative is of paramount importance. . . . The initiative is not something which is handed over on a plate; it has to be consciously fought for and won." These tactical considerations, which correspond exactly to Groulx's ideas as to the kind of war that should have been waged by the *Patriotes*, were written by Mao Tse-Tung. Vladimir Dedijer, one of Tito's companions-in-arms, describes the tactics adopted by the Yugoslavian partisans in the following terms: "Our tactics consisted of attacking the enemy at night, offering the strongest possible resistance, but refusing to accept a frontal battle, and destroying all communications" [Vladimir Dedijer, *Tito Speaks* (London: Weidenfeld and Nicolson, 1953), p. 182]. Lionel Groulx's "irregular warfare" is an invention of the underdog: it is not a magic recipe but the multifaceted and unpredictable expression of the desire to stay alive on the part of a group lacking arms and ammunition and short on strength and organization. Guerilla warfare is nothing more than the infinitely repeated act of cunning of a group which enters into a combat for which it is not yet ready. As Pierre Dalloz wrote of a Maquis counter-offensive in occupied France, "it must be done by surprise and against a distressed and disorganized enemy. . . . It will not be a matter of attacking an enemy in full possession of his resources, but of intervening to aggravate his disorder. . . . It will not be a matter of holding out, but of driving forward in all directions." [Robert Aron, *France Reborn. The History of the Liberation, June 1944–May 1945*, trans. Humphrey Hare (New York: Charles Scribner's Sons, 1964), pp. 188–89.]

7. Dr. Wolfred Nelson, the *Patriotes'* military leader at St. Denis, was later exiled by Durham to Bermuda. Elected to the legislative assembly in 1831, Jean-Joseph Girouard was a leading reformer but a somewhat reluctant soldier; he was imprisoned for seven months in 1837–38. Dr. Jean-Olivier Chénier was killed in action at St. Eustache, where he had taken command of the insurgents. (*Ed.*)

8. Mao Tse-Tung, *Selected Works* (London: Lawrence & Wishart, 1954), vol. I, p. 233.

9. Ibid., p. 206.

10. The *Chasseurs* were an underground resistance movement, formed in 1838 in preparation for an invasion organized by those *Patriotes* exiled in the United States. (*Ed.*)

11. Charles Hindenlang and P. Touvrey were French mercenaries. Hindenlang became Brigadier of the *Chasseur* forces at Napierville and, along with Robert Nelson and Ménard Hébert, led the rebel troops at Odelltown, 9 November 1838. He was hanged 15 February 1839, for his part in the rebellion. One of the Polish officers mentioned here was Colonel Oklowski, who took over the command of the insurgents from Touvrey at the battle of Lacolle. (*Ed.*)

12. Dr. Robert Nelson, younger brother of Wolfred Nelson, supported Papineau in the legislative assembly but did not take part in the 1837 uprising. However, he joined

those rebels who were in exile in the United States and played an important role in the events of 1838. In February of that year he entered Canada, planted a tree of liberty and proclaimed himself president of the Republic. Chevalier de Lorimier was involved in both rebellions and was one of twelve insurgents who were hanged 15 February 1839, after a court martial. (*Ed.*)

13. The following articles are excerpted from the proclamation made by the provisional government in 1838: "WE SOLEMNLY DECLARE: I. That from this day forward the People of Lower Canada are absolved from any allegiance to Great Britain... II. That Lower Canada shall assume a Republican form of government and is now declared, de facto, a Republic. III. That... all citizens shall have the same rights, and that Indians shall enjoy the same rights as others... IV. That any union between Church and State is declared abolished... V. That feudal tenure is, de facto, abolished... " And so on. The proclamation of 1838 sets out, in 18 paragraphs, its political principles. The document was signed by the president of the provisional government, Robert Nelson.

The Differential Calculus of Counter-Revolution

F IRST THEOREM: counter-revolution, by definition, comes after a revolution or an attempted revolution.

SECOND THEOREM: the square of the counter-revolution is equal to the square of the revolutionary hypotenuse. Which implies a rational consequence that we shall call, according to custom, a corollary.

COROLLARY: counter-revolution can thus be reduced to a function (among many others) of revolution. Which is another way of saying that any counter-revolution (or reaction) presupposes a preexisting revolutionary datum, whatever its coefficient of success. And that is where we have to make distinctions. Not only should we record the coefficient of success, N1, of each revolutionary datum, but we also need a coefficient, N2, the value of which cannot be verified. The coefficient N2 is a datum which is distinctly resistant to any mathematical transposition and even to any kind of prediction, sociographical or other; but it is this coefficient N2—subject to all those subjective interpretations which,

as we know, give the operation a somewhat pejorative connotation—
that allows us to measure more adequately the exact magnitude of the
counter-revolution.

Using these prolegomena that we have formulated in accordance
with the aesthetics of theorems, we can always attempt—to the best of
our knowledge and despite our being bogged down in subjectivity (a
fact which undoubtedly plays havoc with the reader's attention, even
though he should normally understand that thought ultimately gains a
great deal from revealing its prejudices rather than pretending they do
not exist)—to evaluate the counter-revolutionary or reactionary phenomenon which appears to be taking place in Quebec at the moment
(May-June 1965). We shall not be asking ourselves whether or not
Quebec is going through a crisis of regression (insofar as revolution is
nominally defined as a form of progress!); we are postulating from the
outset that signs of reaction are increasingly evident in Quebec. How
are we to assess these signs? Can we isolate certain "differential" factors and thereby calculate the extent of the reaction as exactly as possible? That is what we are going to try to do.

First, if we are to be logical with our working hypotheses, let us try
to identify the revolution and formulate it in terms of an equation. Out
of respect for reality it would seem more fitting to use the term "revolutionary datum" rather than "revolution" which, in the full sense of the
word, concerns only those revolutions of which the coefficient of success is, mathematically speaking, absolute. The "revolutionary datum" which gives rise to the reaction we are studying is afflicted—if we
may use that term—with a coefficient of success close to zero, hence
with an optimum coefficient of failure that is to be regarded as a coefficient of passivity or negativity; in short, were it not for other factors
working against it, this coefficient of failure, which to this day characterizes the revolutionary datum in Quebec, would be sufficient to can-
cel that datum out entirely. To the extent that the coefficient of failure
acts as an inhibiting factor, the coefficient N2 (of threatening potential-
ity) can be measured in terms of duration of impact and intensity of in-
ference; moreover, without these factors it would be impossible for
anyone to understand, let alone endorse, a plan of counter-revolution.
Let us start with the intensity of action of the coefficient N2, which has
been in a state of almost constant decline since its high point (which actually dates from the month of March 1963 when the FLQ was propi-
tiously shrouded in mystery and operating at full power). This inten-

sity, despite the fact that it has been declining for the past two years, seems to have kept the driving qualities which define it, even if these have become potential in nature; it might be said, by way of analogy, that the intensity of impact has undergone, at most, a semantic slippage (of a metonymic kind) which has minimized its present visibility even more than its potential, which is assumed to be more unpredictable and hence, as it were, more threatening. The duration of its impact has in no way suffered, for the "dismantling of the FLQ" has increased the fears of many counter-revolutionaries, who identify the resurgence of terrorism with their own surprise and conclude, from the "apparent" calm which reigns in the land, that there is an increased possibility of conspiracy, more secret and perhaps even more determined than the kind announced by outbursts of violence in their peaceful lives. This anxiety, which has taken the place of a terror which can be verified in terms of events, is a very active factor which contributes —all the more effectively since it goes in disguise—to a resurgence of revolutionary acts.

The coefficient N2 approaches infinity, which, as everyone knows, inspires as much terror as fascination. It is also easy to calculate, being inversely proportional to the coefficient of success. Which is to say that a revolution that accomplishes what it sets out to do (i.e., that succeeds) has a depressing effect on the anxiety factor N2.

As can be seen from my calculations, in cases where success is not forthcoming revolution equals a fantasy of revolution and does not lend itself at all well to matters of petty bookkeeping; strictly speaking, it is something which cannot be calculated, yet which is the object of the most basely calculating attentions. This property of incommensurability takes us into a new and as yet unknown branch of mathematics. Something which cannot be calculated can be the object of an exact description as an incalculable phenomenon: what gives the revolution its imperceptible quality can thus be the object of a phenomenological description of the "continuum" of any revolutionary datum. Under the mask of apparent discontinuity can be found a continuous phenomenon.

Continuity is a notion which encompasses many things—even discontinuity which, when all is said and done, can be seen as a flaw in the continuum or even as a fluctuation in the index of continuity. As we know, the Einsteinian continuum promotes viscosity and stickiness; calculating reality in terms of continuity really makes you feel part of the dirty, silt-laden tide of Bergsonian intuition. How can one swim free of it? How can one extricate oneself from this uninterrupted tide of seminal intuition? Teilhard de Chardin's never-ending genesis has something glutinous about it; one would like to be able to pull the lever marked "counter-genesis" and shed more light on things by interrupting the sticky, polluted flow of this river of ultra-continuity; one would like to make it change beds or halt its flow with a wall of cement, give it falls to contend with or even dry it up. The irreversible continuity of history must be reversible, otherwise I frankly pity those who are outside the continuum, unbalanced (historically speaking), exposed to the disrupting oscillations of the discontinuous.

In fact, there is no such thing as unilateral or linear continuity, any more than there is such a thing as absolute progress. (Remember that Genesis was followed quite closely by the Flood, a singularly violent counter-genesis. As an archetype of all phenomena of discontinuity, the Flood represents neither more nor less than the Hegelian antithesis.)

Let us not go thinking that History is a grand symphonic piece with themes, sub-themes, reprises and polyphonic continuity. History, which mires Hegel and Bergson with the same mud, is much more like armed combat, never ending since at irregular intervals a new battalion will loom suddenly out of the thick mist, sabres drawn, to charge the soft, pale flank of continuity. I think (at last!) I'm getting warm: yes, I'm on the verge of understanding the secret structure of the historical process. I can see clearly in my heart; the differential calculus releases within me a flood of brutal joy and of course, above all, a stream of lucidity. This, dear reader, is my reward, and yours too (yes, I am going to let you in on my secret): discontinuity is continuous, which is another way of saying that, as you have perhaps guessed, the currency of continuity is discontinuity.

All of a sudden I have an attack of incalculable hiccoughs which give me a faint idea of the sway of discontinuity over continuity. This final hiccough leaves me panting with intelligence: discontinuity is continuous, therefore the revolution is permanent and the counter-revolution (be it ever so quiet) is a comma. Period.

["Calcul différentiel de la contre-révolution."
Liberté VII, no. 3 (May-June 1965): 272–75.]

Literature and Alienation

The notion of alienation is one of those overused concepts which clutter up our vocabulary. Alienation sometimes describes the feeling of emptiness which follows a stint of work; socially, it refers to a lack of autonomy or a group's colonized or inferior status. And of course, it must not be forgotten that the word has long been used as a general term for mental illness.

We can deduce from this that alienation implies a certain deprivation: one is deprived of one's rights, one's freedom, one's sanity.

I have always thought that there was a certain ambiguity in the application of this notion to literature, since it implies that literary production is a compensatory activity in our society and that writers enjoy exactly the same status as the mentally ill. According to this view, the writer would be a kind of ideal madman, abandoning himself to his wild imaginings while everyone else is involved in "serious" production.

In fact, the writer is marginal and feels marginal in our hyper-industrialized society. We are vaguely aware that every society has its writers and that, in this respect, our own society is no exception to this calamitous rule. According to this unwritten philosophy, literature represents a contingency or a superfluous decoration. Literary activity, stigmatized as unimportant and pointless, loses its value; and as for the writer, he is defined as someone who relies on symbols to overcome his own alienation (or sometimes that of his group). Now I object to this ideology (if that is not too grand a term) that belittles literature by claiming that its function is to express what is alienated or to compensate for that alienation.

I have no hesitation in stating with conviction an opposing point of view: that of art for art's sake. I am asserting that literature is neither a function nor the reflection of an alienation: writers are free, and I willingly recognize their freedom to write for writing's sake, just as I recognize the right of musicians and artists to use non-representational forms. If, nowadays, we accept non-figurative art, we should by the same token allow that literature too can be "non-figurative."

Of course, literary production is unthinkable without consumers—I mean, without readers, without an audience. But that does not mean to say that one can invoke the necessity of that audience in order to infer from it that the writer is bound by that transaction and that he has to meet a requirement of meaningfulness. That argument is not consistent. Literature has a coefficient of meaning which is progressively diminishing as the centuries go by. One can say—quite matter of factly—that Homer's *Odyssey* was packed with meaning whereas its modern version, Joyce's *Ulysses*, is laden with more incoherence than meaning. A comparison of these two monumental works allows us at least to observe that, over a period of some two thousand years, the literary product has gained in autonomy what it has lost in meaning. It means less and less, but is more and more comparable to a painting or a consciously crafted work of art. The many interpretations given of Joyce's *Ulysses* show indirectly that the proliferation of signs is a technical device or, if you prefer, a decorative way of presenting a story. This plurality of conflicting meanings detracts from the idea of a book's single, unifying meaning and makes literature lean towards "non-figurative" art.

Is it possible to get the message across that Joyce, with all his hotchpotch of novel techniques and his arsenal of defused English words, is our master, our sole, abominable professor of disproportion, completely unbalanced, our only guide? That's right—it is Joyce, our breathtaking brother, who wields our uncertain pen, urging us on to write insanities for the sole purpose of writing insanities. Of course, that concerns me; in fact, we are the only ones it does concern, me and the other poor jokers who go on lining up words one after the other in order to break the sordid fascination that binds us to other people's normality. Joyce is not one of us; and yet, in his death, he is a brother of ours... and I know that some of us make the trip to Zurich to visit what is left of him: the invisible body, buried six feet under, of a friend who died on foreign soil but who had time before his death to light the fuse and plot to the last detail the explosion of all the meanings of the words he juggled and all the connotations of a language which had but one shortcoming: that it was not his native tongue. After all, why not Zurich? A Catholic cemetery, in the fortified heart of Zwingli, has all the charm of a *petitio principii* or of an enormous farce...

At this stage, literature has to find other ways of catching the reader's attention than by bombarding him with messages and dictating to him word by word an unimpeachable version of life.... The novel has already started to explode like an old shack that has had an H-bomb smuggled into it. There is no narration any more, no more narrative structure, no chronological order or story. Novelists are paid to know that they have to present their novels outside any narrative tradition and according to new norms that are appropriate to what is being written and to the times in which we live. The last century had its quarrels over "art for art's sake"; now everything has gone by the boards. Art is finally free and the artist no longer feels bound by the transmission of meaning. The writer is alienated by the idea of a message to be delivered; his freedom of invention suffers and he finds himself domesticated and transformed by society into a function. He is reduced to expressing his feelings and to making books which represent the world. Nothing is more damaging or more impoverishing than this functionalization of literature. In those countries that are under Soviet domination, literature can be said to be dying of being nothing more than an instrument and the writer merely an official bard. One might as well say that in those societies literature is assassinated before it comes into being... and that it is an absolute miracle if it gives the odd sign of survival. In the other arts Soviet controls were every bit as disastrous. And if there is any doubt, one only has to recall the horror that was the infamous "Soviet realism."

Michelangelo and Bernini, despite the fact that they were entirely dependent on popes and princes, were freer than those artists who are compelled to work in the name of an ideology or a party. And Pasternak? Well, let us be frank: Pasternak's work is not worth very much in comparison with that of Balzac, Faulkner, Proust, Joyce or Capote. His success in the West is probably attributable to the assumption that novels produced behind the Iron Curtain could only be extremely mediocre. Pasternak is the exception that proves the rule: his work is not extremely mediocre but only moderately so.

It will perhaps be thought that I am being unfair. But, unfair or not, I have no qualms about loathing Pasternak, to whom the Quebec Ministry of Cultural Affairs (Creative Writing Programme) would not have given a grant of a thousand dollars. As a writer, he was too lazy to sell out. . . instead, he gave himself away. What he produced does not annoy me, it disgusts me; to such an extent that I do not even feel the desire, or the need, to justify my feelings of nausea. For me, there is not the slightest shadow of a doubt: Pasternak found inspiration only in the most distressing servility. In exchange for a *dacha* in the suburbs and a pathetic salary, he wrote what is nothing more than a sinister parody of a work of art. If he had had any sense of honour left, he might have been enterprising enough to commit suicide; but there again, for that he would have needed an ounce of lucidity. Pasternak had all the qualities of a kept writer, except one: he was happy with his fate; he cherished his wonderful Soviet security and his little *dacha:* he died there, full of his ludicrous fame and in keeping with the mediocrity of the false patriot, which he had in abundance. If I had to express myself at greater length on the subject, I would have an irresistible urge to say nothing. For simple-mindedness (sheer charlatanism) inclines me to silence and, beyond that, to the worst blasphemies that for us here in Quebec are our excuse for a national heritage.

But it is not just in the Soviet bloc that the writer is alienated. There is a literary tradition which weighs heavy on today's writers, and that is the concept of the writer's role. That role exists of course, but it is generally reduced to one of expression and meaning. Now, nothing is more restrictive than this limitation. This conception of the writer's role is as anachronistic as the tradition that says that a novel has to tell a story and be composed according to the laws of narrative. The writer who accepts this pernicious precept, which is dictated to him *sub rosa* by an entire society, falls headlong into a trap. He is had in the full sense of the word, trapped in the most unimaginative and meaningless conformity. Now *there* is an example of literary alienation!

As for writers who come from alienated peoples, they can hold up to shame the alienation from which their brothers suffer. But as artists, they are depriving themselves of their freedom if they confine themselves to being nothing more than mouthpieces for that collective alienation. And in those circumstances, the literature they produce is degraded, impoverished, impaired. Without realizing it, they write nationalist novels—just like the regionalist novels of another era. And, let's face it, such novels are written to expound a thesis and derive their form from the most hackneyed traditions of fiction.

Unfortunately, I have no more sympathy for certain Quebec writers who advocate the systematic use of *joual* in literature. It could be said that *joual* is a relatively contaminated or damaged form of speech. It has been regarded by certain writers as the true language used by real Québécois to communicate with one another. But that is not the case; this so-called vernacular *joual* is a fraud concocted by writers who sincerely believe in the liberating powers of a literature of derision. According to these precepts, literature in *joual* is a first step in the process of decolonization. It is my opinion that the whole idea of literature in *joual* rests on a misapprehension: the form of speech that these writers see as being the norm in Quebec is in fact not very widespread at all and is even in a state of decline. Literature in *joual* leads directly to an impasse: it is the literature of non-communication, a literature without a future, lacking in formal resources and in formal possibilities.

Of course, the French spoken in Quebec has its own idioms, like the French that is spoken in the francophone cantons of Switzerland, or in Belgium or in the French-speaking countries of Black Africa. As we know, these regional forms of a language spoken in different parts of the world are normal and give no cause for concern insofar as the populations of these various countries are relatively large, geographically concentrated and politically structured. That is true of the more than six million French-speaking inhabitants of Quebec, whose taxes go to maintain a government the importance and autonomy of which have been established for decades. The Government of Quebec is French-speaking: it passes laws in French and actively promotes an education system in which French has pride of place. Which undoubtedly explains why French (even in spite of certain accents or certain idioms) is making lasting progress in Quebec. In other words, this intensive French schooling tends to make the French spoken in Quebec more uniform and even more international. But I am far from advocating that our patterns of speech should be entirely modelled on the Parisian accent.

As a writer I feel free, when it suits me, to use words or expressions which are typical of Quebec French. After all, I am using a living language. . . . But I am far from being tempted to think that *joual* is a language; it is a dialect, at times picturesque but poor when used exclusively, as certain writers tend to use it. Literature written in *joual* (and only in *joual*) will date rapidly. The writers from the Liège area who, around 1880, produced works in their dialect or patois met the same sad fate.

It must not be forgotten that French is just as much our language as that of France; and Quebec writers are increasingly aware that, like their French counterparts, they are using a comprehensible, living language.

I am well aware that it is difficult for me to be objective when it comes to my own experience as a writer; but even so, that does not stop me from speaking out frankly and saying that it gives me great joy to produce novels written in French for a French-speaking public, but also destined to carry the desperate enormity of my plots beyond the borders of Quebec. There emerge in this way, not the misty contours of my brain, but the uncertain frontiers of my country which extend infinitely and interminably beyond the native soil that they enclose. Goodbye to objectivity! Goodbye to the infamous federal objectivity. Goodbye forever to something that looks remarkably like the absolutist dogma of a fixed and finished earth: Galileo went that route and now, far behind, here am I, following modestly in his footsteps. It is not just the earth that turns, it is our native land that is set in motion and that other country, the false one that is kept under the federal shroud, that is exploding and crumbling. I am a writer: nothing but a Quebec writer whose sole function is to go on producing multiple versions of an "odyssey" which, from sea to rocks, takes an uncomplicated hero by way of Charybdis to Scylla, but will also in the end bring him back to the port of Ithaca, the lugubrious haven of the St. Lawrence. One day the wandering Québécois will have finished his unbearable odyssey: he is already worn out with the attempt to reach his home port; he wants

to be done with it; I can feel him straining inside me, dictating the uncertain route of his final voyage, of his homecoming. The Plains of
Abraham fade slowly away in the enemy mist; they grow dim, slipping,
little by little, lethally down towards the black river which flows on
without rest or season. Yes, they are done with, the Plains of Abraham:
they can no longer find a buyer or a soldier capable of crossing them en
route to conquest. This military business is no longer an honest man's
sport: the famous plains are crumpled like paper, torn up like love letters never sent. Everything is at half-mast in Quebec and will stay that
way until the phantom patriot, dressed up as a writer, wraithlike
wends his way home. Outside this collective obsession, which is as
close as we come to hope and happiness, no other plot is possible any
more.

The same cannot be said for the Franco-Canadian groups scattered
through the other provinces of Canada. Their future as linguistic
minorities does not look good; with the possible exception of the
Franco-Ontarians from around Sudbury or Sturgeon Falls and maybe,
at a pinch, the Acadians from New Brunswick, they are generally out of
phase with their surroundings. These scattered groups no longer have
any real status and seem to be on the road to linguistic extinction. The
assimilation rate bears witness to their plight. They are in the same
boat as the Doukhobors. They are slowly fading away; which is, sadly,
the way of things.

Needless to say, I do not believe in bilingualism or in pan-Canadian
biculturalism. The literary output (not to speak of other forms of productivity) of isolated bilingual groups is virtually nonexistent. The coming to power at the head of the anglophone federal government of
someone who is presumed to be a French Canadian is comparable to
the election of a Black Power representative to the White House. The
present prime minister is a living embodiment of alienation. Is it think-
able, for example, that an English Canadian should be elected premier
of Quebec? Yet it would be scarcely more anomalous.

The literature of Quebec is not out of phase with the literature produced in France, or indeed in other countries. Now that Quebec writers
and artists have become aware of their identity, they show a formal
vitality which is pretty impressive. The old artistic canons are being
broken wide open and will go on being so in Quebec. And this effront-
ery does not date from yesterday. The revolutionary tradition in
Quebec art and literature goes back to the 1948 publication, in St.

Hilaire, of a little book called *Refus global*. This booklet, of which only 400 copies were printed, was the work of the painter Paul-Émile Borduas and his group. Its inflammatory pages triggered a desire for liberation amongst Quebec artists that is still alive and well in the latest poems of Paul Chamberland or Gaston Miron, or in the novels of Jacques Godbout and the violent works of Marie-Claire Blais. It would be difficult to speak here of influence in the strict sense of the word, since I am not certain that the writers I have just mentioned are familiar with the actual text of *Refus global*; we ought rather to speak of a secret kinship or an unconscious line of descent. Witness for example this passage from *Refus global* which one might easily confuse with the trenchant lyricism of some of Miron's poems:

The frontiers of our dreams are no longer the same.

Or this:

Break once and for all with all society's customs, dissociate oneself from its utilitarian outlook. . . . Refuse to be confined to the ghetto of the plastic arts, which is difficult to storm but too easy to pass by. Refuse to remain silent. . . . Refuse to serve, to be used. . . .
Make way for magic! Make way for objective mysteries!
Make way for love!
Make way for necessities!

And here are the closing lines of Borduas' cry from the heart:

Let those who are tempted by adventure join us.
We can imagine a future in which man, freed from his idle chains, will realize, in a necessarily spontaneous and unpredictable way, in glorious anarchy, the full potential of his individual talents.
Until then. . . we will joyfully pursue our unbridled lust for liberation.

Borduas gave as it were the signal for an artistic revolution which even today finds an echo in the best plastic and literary creations in Quebec. Published in 1948, this little book is important for an understanding of the general explosion taking place in all the arts in Quebec.

It is the first step in the long process of revising our goals upward. This literature—which had once been dead or too concerned with not doing anything new—is already displaying a richness and an assurance that a Crémazie, a Fréchette or a Ringuet never dreamed of attaining. Those writers of another age are perfect examples of a national and personal alienation for which they did not even have a name. But now the un- nameable has been named, described, analyzed, lived, and lived over again. So much the better!

We are no longer writing solely to compensate for a defective reality or to exorcise a collective alienation of which all Québécois are thought to be possessed. Of course, every Quebec writer is aware of the social and political situation of his people; and he knows very well that his people are fighting to free themselves fully and truly from Ottawa's tutelage. But this determination, shared by a great number of Québéc- ois, is a source more of exaltation than of alienation. And when every- thing in a society explodes, it is perhaps predictable and even normal that literature should explode at the same time and free itself from all formal or social constraints. Now that Borduas is dead, the call for freedom that he put out in 1948 has grown louder. Borduas planted the first bomb under our society's structures, thereby reviving the memory of the revolution of 1837–1838. That revolution is still brewing un- derground and in the books that are being written in Quebec. It has lib- erating virtues which tend to be infectious.

Laval, Quebec.

["Littérature et aliénation." *Mosaic* II, no. 1 (Fall 1968): 45–52.]

The Death of the Accursed Writer

I am here, I imagine, at this Seventh Meeting of damned writers,[1] for the sole purpose of putting on a fantastic show—a sort of total performance, so to speak—starring a writer who is not just accursed but mythical to boot, and featuring a cast of fellow writers, readers, analysts, fallen women and men of the world. According to the theoretical materials which were distributed before the panel discussion, it would seem that the accursed writer is a kind of myth which, through the effects of marketing and exposure, is becoming out of date—or something along those lines, something... reactionary. I have taken the liberty of deducing from the inaugural (or simply augural) address that the accursed writer would be wise—if he wants to keep abreast of the times and not find himself excluded or, worse, consigned to the scrap heap—to arrange his immediate demise.

But what exactly is an accursed writer? According to this panel's prospectus, as a poet he cuts a sombre figure, Faust-like, tragic, but above all inspired. . . and, by virtue of that very inspiration, inclined to downplay the importance of the work of conscious fashioning involved in his creations.

He also represents, much as we would like to deny it, a certain image of the writer as sacred. According to this imagery, he is invested with a sort of occult power, subject to blinding flashes of what is thought to be inspiration, a kind of innate spontaneity over which he has no control and which spills out as if by magic from left to right on the paper.

I believe it is vital that the notion of unconscious inspiration lose its special status as something holy; I do not, however, think that literary production should be demystified for the sake of attaining something which exists outside the artificiality peculiar to literature.

On the contrary, I am advocating that we canonize precisely that artificiality which, in my opinion, is intrinsic to anything that is written; so that that artificiality, once it became conscious, might reveal the most important characteristic of the literary artefact—the writer's technique.

Seen in this light, literature becomes an exchange between reader and writer—an exchange which reflects the extent of the reader's involvement and understanding. In which case, one might as well expunge the term "accursed writer" from the language. We have to understand that the writer can only appear accursed from the point of view of a reader who is intimidated by the various methods and devices used by the writer. One is tempted to think that behind the "accursed writer" concept there lies a prejudice which sees the production of works of literature as going hand in hand with a certain abnormality. Which leads to anything that seems abnormal being characterized as accursed; and from there to regarding what is accursed as being inaccessible is only a step away—a step which is quickly taken.

Is the accursed writer dead? It seems to me that the very title of this morning's discussion shows that its authors have given an implicit but at the same time ambiguous answer to that question. The death of the accursed writer—such an equivocal statement, half affirmation and half pious hope, postulating in one breath the death of the accursed writer and in the next implicitly assuming that he has not yet given up the ghost.

If I am looking for meaning in the wording of a title, it is probably because I think that not much was left to chance in the choice of that title and that I ought to be able to find an intention, however vague, behind that little screen of fine words.

Can that hidden intention escape a methodical analysis? I think not. (And I hope that no one feels unfairly singled out by my curiosity.) Well, this is what that title phrase says to me:

1) firstly, that the writer (and I am happy to let the epithet drop) is dead;

2) secondly, that the writer is cursed (and cursing) because he is not dead;

3) thirdly, that one can conclude from this: a) that the writer is thought to be destined for a specific and irreversible death, and b) that he is openly cursed for not conforming to the desire expressed in a).

In short, the title phrase contains two mutually exclusive assumptions which could be formulated as follows: either death or damnation... but not both at once; that would be, so to speak, too perfect.

Now that I have, to my own satisfaction at least, taken apart the image of the accursed writer, all that remains is for me confess where I stand in this business. Do I see myself as cursed or not? At least I can force a description out of myself in this respect—a matter of seeing clearly in total darkness.

I do believe myself to be cursed, to be the object of certain maledictions (quite honestly); but I think I understand that the curse which attaches to me as a writer is not a unilateral, irreversible, implacable condemnation. God knows, the unilateral and the simple are growing rarer and rarer these days and in our society! (Which is all for the good: complexity and ambiguity reassure me that people are serious.) But to come back to me, as they say. The accursed writer (in the Quebec of 1969) is simply the embodiment of the ambiguous vocation of the people of Quebec—a people who are themselves at once cursed and welcomed, evil and beneficent, dangerous, terrible and accepted.

It would embarrass me to say that, as a writer, I embody the uncertain vocation of the Quebec nation, for there is nothing messianic about me, nothing on that scale. Above me and far ahead of me I would place, for example, a Gaston Miron whose exemplary calling has something stunning and absolutely wonderful about it. Just as he stands, he is our Christ. And I think that it is a tribute to him when I say that, more and more, the mere mention of his name constitutes an extraordinary act of blasphemy.

Before him, if my memory serves me well, only a Louis-Joseph Papineau attained such an explosively blasphemous status. But it has been a long time. And then, it must be said in his defence that dear old Papineau lived at a time when the English would stamp on us without batting an eyelid. A devil of a man, at once the idol and the terror of his people, his name was a curse, an incitement to riot. Among us here, in 1969, Louis-Joseph Papineau would likely meet the same kind of wretched fate as that reserved, for example, for an André Laurendeau.[2]

In other words, there has been a shift in the level of malediction, which I would now say seems to require a Gaston Miron. For me, this man is a model, an eternally exhilarating example of what in our society—which, as everyone knows, is founded on the national condensation of holy water—is accursed.

The accursed writer is certainly damned; but he is not dead, thank God (or thank the devil).

Whatever the message of a Quebec writer, whatever the contents of a book or a piece of writing, he finds himself faced, in spite of himself, with the following problem: how to invent a new way of being Québécois through the writing of books. Not that he should take it into his head to represent or reflect the Quebec society that he sees around him (we are not mirrors); but by virtue of his Quebec roots, he will probably have no choice but to be blatantly Québécois, to create his personal mode of revelation and invent the style of his own epiphany, in order to be (in his books) so Québécois that it will make you want to throw up.

I hope I have been properly understood: I am not advocating some kind of typicality or representativeness that every Quebec writer must assume in his work. I am simply saying that it is not easy to be Québécois and that this fact is reflected in the literature that is produced in Quebec just as it is in other kinds of activity. To be Québécois in a lukewarm way has disastrous consequences—witness the pathetic MPs and ministers who represent us in Ottawa. In literature, too, the results are painful. (Would my drift be clear if I were to spit in passing on a Pierre Trottier?)[3]

I maintain, against all likelihood, that I am a living writer; and I am going to carry on—insofar as I can follow through on this plan of existence—writing increasingly futile variations on the nothingness of which we writers are the indomitable embodiment. Our endeavour can be compared to an attempt—of uncertain appeal—to give form to an inner vacuity which, by that very fact, we take a certain pleasure in flaunting, in the hope that our potential readers will also find a certain pleasure therein.

The Argentinian writer, Borges, has said: "Reading is, for the moment, an act which comes after that of writing, an act which is more daring, more courteous, more intellectual."

"More courteous"... Borges's word seems to me very apt to describe the act of reading. According to this way of looking at things, it is logical to see in the writer's endeavour a lack of respect, an impropriety. I am inclined to be in full agreement with Jorge Luis Borges and his splendid conception of courtesy and discourtesy (reading and writing). And as Borges is logical, he often goes so far as to reduce the act of writing to an esoteric prospecting of the "total library" to which we all have access, inasmuch as we have sufficient patience and sufficient method to explore it thoroughly and incessantly.

It is quite inappropriate to close on such a hermetic note when one has set out to talk about THE DEATH OF THE ACCURSED WRITER. But I get tangled up in the interlace of Borges's prose, enjoying it even, shamelessly adopting his undemonstrable suppositions and his "indiscernible identities" (a principle he has taken, by the way, from Leibnitz). The accursed writer is fortunately one who is short on courtesy, who bristles at any blessing, and who disputes the beneficial effects of holy water.[4] By contrast, the blessed writer is the spitting image of that water, which has flowed for two centuries and more in our conquered veins.

To paraphrase my favourite writer, Paracelsus (or Philippus Aureolus Theophrastus Bombastus von Hohenheim), who said that man was a condensed mist, I would submit that the accursed writer is nothing but a condensed mist of holy water. You will say that, well... after all... Paracelsus... Very well, but let me say once and for all and in all seriousness that Paracelsus—even more so than Borges—is my Doppelgänger.

["La mort de l'écrivain maudit." Liberté XI, no. 3–4 (May-June-July 1969): 26–31.]

Editor's Notes

1. This essay was given as a paper at the Seventh Meeting of Writers (VIIe Rencontre des Écrivains), organized by the journal *Liberté* and held in Ste. Adèle, May 29-June 1, 1969. The general title of the conference was "The Writer, Literature and the Mass Media" and the first morning was devoted to four papers on "The Death of the Accursed Writer" ("La mort de l'écrivain maudit") given by Marcel Saint-Pierre, Pierre Pagé, Robert Melançon and Aquin.
2. André Laurendeau (see also "The Mystic Body") had died in 1968. As a French-Canadian nationalist committed to a humane and equitable bicultural and bilingual Canada, his vision was necessarily at odds with Aquin's passionately separatist views.
3. Pierre Trottier is apparently singled out here by Aquin because of his long association with the federal government and, more particularly, the Ministry of External Affairs. A globe-trotting career diplomat, Trottier had won the Prix David in 1960 for his poetry.
4. The French reads: ". . . celui qui conteste la validité bénéfique du goupillon." *Goupillon* refers to the aspergillum, used to sprinkle the faithful with holy water; the term had come to stand symbolically for the despotic powers of the Catholic Church during the Duplessis era. In *Refus global*, Borduas had exclaimed: "Au diable le goupillon et la tuque!"—a cry echoed in Michèle Lalonde's essay, "Entre le goupillon et la tuque," translated by Larry Shouldice as "The Mitre and the Tuque," in *Contemporary Quebec Criticism* (Toronto: University of Toronto Press, 1979), pp. 83–92.

Thoughts on the Status of the Writer

M ore and more I have the feeling that the only way the writer can find favour in the eyes of the public is by justifying his existence, with supporting documentation, through extra-literary activities. That is an irrefutable fact which none of us can escape, no matter how many copies we sell—at least in Quebec and Canada.

Some become polygraphs, writing for television; others (myself included) become professors. But I don't know of any who have the courage to be writers to the end, making no concessions to the social system in which we live—I mean, without working for television or having some high-ranking civil service position in Quebec City or Ottawa; without heading (as they say) some library or teaching in a college or university. And this is the norm; in France, too, I know, except of course for the literary superstars who break every sales record in the book (Sartre or Françoise Sagan...).

My readers are perhaps thinking at this very moment that I am complaining, but that is not the case; in describing the situation, I am not passing sentence on it. Paradoxically, the society that seems to be so mean with its writers only makes them feel more a part of that society than they would probably be if they were comfortably looked after. Which is not to say that writers should be in some way institutionally penalized in order to make them give of their best; I am even tempted to think the opposite. The possibility of making a living through literature seems to me to be the best way of boosting productivity.

But the problem is there (or not too far away). The possibility of turning a profit must not be artificially created; it has to be genuine, real, sufficient. And that is not yet the case. At least, there have not emerged in the general population, in Quebec or in Canada, any real pools of readers capable of the amount of literary consumption that would allow authors to live off their royalties. On the other hand, both Quebec and Canada have put in place institutional mechanisms for financial compensation: grants, subsidies, support for creative writing, numerous prizes.

Now, the most modest of writers—the one who is least apt to convince the reading public to read him—is still eligible for a very large number of grants which, as it were, give him the illusion that society is bestowing upon him a lot of money and, in so doing, conferring great merit upon him. What is truly paradoxical is that this situation—which is "socialist" in principle—turns out to be a simple capitalist stimulant designed to keep the subsidized writer in a particular state of euphoric conformity in respect to society. It is enough for certain writers to become depoliticized for them to receive these kinds of false rewards, which in fact bear no more relation to their true value than to their public appeal. I would not go so far as to say that the system of subsidies to creative artists is a bad system; far be it from me to say such a thing. I simply believe that writers who are supported in this way are really only kept afloat by artificial means. The grants and subsidies they receive will never replace genuine, bona fide popularity, which turns a profit.

And when I say popularity, I am not restricting the writer to the success of his works alone; I am thinking rather of the response to him as a person, as a real living presence, and his ability to give voice in different ways to the concerns of others. The writer is certainly not a specialist in grammar, but rather a specialist in using words. His value is intimately bound up with the value of what he formulates—orally or in writing—for others or in front of others; this process of formulation even constitutes the chief activity of the writer. He writes, formulates, reports, designates and defines, playing with words and those bits of reality that interest him, constantly manipulating small or large units of words and phrases, sense and nonsense. For even if he is defined by the act of formulation, we must not jump to the conclusion that that forces him to make constant sense; on the contrary, he can be just as much at home in the irresponsible splendour of words and the gratuitous in-consequentiality of fiction. There is nothing in law to oblige someone who writes or speaks to do so in accordance with an established pattern of meaning. There is nothing, for example, to oblige me to bring what I have started to a harmonious conclusion... any more than the reader is obliged to hear me out until the last of my wild imaginings has tortuously percolated. And this point of law grants total, retroactive immunity to everything that is commonly written, said, formulated and read. Even the fiction which is the most monstrously detached from his-torical truth (if it is even possible to speak of historical truth) is never punishable, which brings me back to where I started. Any formulation must be viewed as really emanating from the person of whoever does the formulating. The popularity I was speaking of a moment ago would be nothing more than a sort of very powerful radiation effect of that phenomenon of emanation.

You are going to tell me that you are on the verge of being convinced by my weird and wonderful pronouncements that I am certifiably in-sane or that I am speaking in tongues. Easy enough to say, but how do you prove it? For perhaps the truth is that I am terribly shy. Or perhaps a kind of businessman, using words to make some vulgar deal. Or worse still, perhaps I am just the shadow of some sinister joker who has taken it into his head to impersonate me and, in the process, make you think I am crazy. A disturbing thought... Am I real? Am I simply a writer who is so horribly Québécois that he goes on and on about the hair he is splitting, while the poor hair placidly allows itself to be evenly sliced in nice, greasy little sections?

It is up to you, dear reader, to make a summary decision; yes, it is for you to pronounce the verdict which will decide how genuine and serious-minded I am. Or perhaps I should say that it is for you rather to sentence me to death by writing (capital punishment if ever there was one...).

But for this once I am inclined to bring my ranting and raving to an abrupt end and close on a harsh note, leaving you with the hope that another time my stock will be on the rise and that that will confer greater value on what I do. . . and on what I am doing, here, in public.[1]

Editor's Note

1. This text dates from September 1969 but was first published in 1977 in *Blocs errati-ques*, pp. 259–61, under the title "Propos sur l'écrivain."

Joual: Haven or Hell?

The debate surrounding the use of *joual* is not a false problem, but it is a sterile one, draining and—it sometimes seems—never-ending. The term *joual* refers to a linguistic divergence which exists between the French we speak and the French of France; and, inasmuch as the bottom of the Atlantic Ocean is not going to rise to the surface to create an unbroken land mass between Gaspé and Finistère, it seems clear to me that a certain linguistic disparity will continue to exist. The divergence is thus variable in intensity and extension but permanent insofar as the basic facts of the matter are concerned.

If *joual* were defined according to what distinguishes our language from English and not according to what differentiates it from French, one would be justified in thinking that *joual* was an indication of the relative anglicization of those who use it. But no! The truth of the matter is that *joual* is a language which, from its origins and throughout its evolution, has defined itself against French. If *joual* does some day

100

emerge as a fully-fledged language, it will figure in the linguistics textbooks as an offshoot of French.

For the time being, *joual* is still in its early stages and is not yet a language; it is a counter-language. It signifies and promotes a subversion of the native language of its advocates, who try to invest it with structures that are independent of the system of the French language. Though there has been no official declaration of war, hostilities are none the less rife. *Joual* is a linguistic resistance movement; and it is not unrealistic to think that what the freedom fighters want to do is to supplant French or even to eradicate it entirely within the borders of Quebec. *Joual* wants to secede from French.

There appears to be an analogy between *joual* and the sovereignty movement. *Joual* is a political programme which defines itself against Confederation or, more or less, against English Canadians. French Canadians are thus the site of a double rejection: rejection of the French language and rejection of the English-dominated federal framework. What is most striking in the conjunction of these two themes is the dream—even unspoken—of a collective parthenogenesis. But I am not interested in developing this kind of symbolic analysis or in demonstrating its validity. I note rather with trepidation that the creative energy of French Canadians is being mobilized against two hegemonies: the hegemony of the French language and the hegemony of the federal government. We therefore have to understand that we are doubly colonized, but by two colonizing entities which have nothing to do with each other, and that our struggle for freedom is taking place on two fronts at once. According to this view of things, the vital forces of the nation are painfully divided.

If I attack *joual* (as a radical desire to constitute a new language, not as a way of speaking French) it is because I see *joual* as a pernicious anaemia; it is not just our language which is affected by it but thought itself, insofar as it is only by being formulated in verbal or written language that thought can come into being. When the formulation is defective, thought becomes embryonic, impotent, dislocated.

There is no shortage of examples of peoples who, following a period of creolization, have ended up adopting a language that is poorer and less effectual than the one they started with. Of course, such instances cannot be reduced to the sum of individual choices; they are collective phenomena which occur over a period longer than a single lifetime. We are not, then, wasting our time in posing the problem of *joual*, inasmuch as the process of instituting this "language" has only just begun. In this instance, passivity on the part of individuals can only favour the collective shift to *joual*.

There are those who will tell me that this shift has already been made and that it is already too late; if that is true, then there is no point worrying about it and I am in complete agreement with the present linguistic divergence between the language spoken in Quebec and the French of France. It has never been my wish to suppress that distance or to eliminate what is peculiarly Québécois about our French; I am even delighted that the distance should be evident and that our national identity should have a unique, distinctive expression.

But if that is the situation, it means that *joual* is simply a metaphorical expression for the French spoken in Quebec. There is nothing in this definition to disturb me, but I know that the advocates of *joual* do not see things in the same way; for them, *joual* will constitute a language distinct from French and English and having all the attributes of a fully-fledged language. Seen in this light, according to Victor-Lévy Beaulieu,[1] works written in *joual* will have to be translated for distribution on the French market.

I said at the beginning of this piece that *joual* is a language which defines itself against French. That statement still seems sound to me; there is, however, another element I want to add to this tentative definition of *joual*. As a French dialect which has been spectacularly contaminated by English, *joual* also constitutes a kind of immunization against anglicizing tendencies, exhibiting a fierce if ambiguous resistance to English. However paradoxical it may seem, *joual* is a bulwark against anglicization inasmuch as it has already absorbed the poison of English; it is hard to imagine anyone slipping from *joual* into English, since the use of *joual* is such a powerful signal that the speaker or writer is Québécois.

The obsession with national identity runs very deep with us, for there are those Québécois who feel threatened with loss of identity if all the ingredients of the national psyche are not strictly Québécois; in other words, they claim that for a nation to express itself totally it has to have a language which is all its own, whereas in fact a people can express itself in a perfectly original way, using a language to which it does not have exclusive rights. A nation can just as well be itself while speaking an international language, although it may mean adapting and enriching that language and providing it with new connotations.

On many occasions during the last few years I have been irritated by the countless debates on the linguistic question in Quebec, for, in my opinion, these debates mask the single most important national problem—the political one. This kind of linguistic squabble between opposing schools of thought crystallizes collective consciousness at secondary levels. The linguistic question is substituted for the national problem and the verbal subversion that is *joual* takes the place of the fight for national liberation. Let me add that verbal subversion does not foster real subversion—it takes its place.

At the same time as we hesitate to give our group an autonomous political framework, we overemphasize our national identity on the level of language. Because they want a self-contained identity which owes as little as possible to what comes from outside, French Canadians practice a permanent cultural subversion which is simply the other face of a permanent colonization. To those who are conquered and who perceive themselves as being conquered, the various forms of subversion come naturally; such people are humiliated, thwarted, irritable and quick to take offence. Cheated and deprived of their rights, they overcompensate by granting themselves the right to political hesitation, the right to indecision, the right to contradict themselves and the right to all rights. The colonized are profoundly ambivalent: they hesitate, they waver and feel guilty for doing so, they always check anything that seems like impulsive behaviour, they are afraid of doing things they might regret and so find themselves constantly on the brink of paralysis. For those who are almost paralyzed, the only form of action is violence and subversion.

When I hear federal minister Gérard Pelletier giving Robert Bourassa a lesson on what it is to be French, I understand that it is the federalists who encourage us to regard our language as being essential and sacred and as having priority. For some time now, there have been efforts by English Canadian federalists to make the French language the object of initiatives of recuperation and revaluation. For let us not forget that French (the second official language) is Canada's trademark.

English Canadians and federalists do not want to give up French, which is part of their heritage and part of the overall image of Canada. However, one cannot hold their fidelity to the federalist ideology against them when they are defending the French language. Federal encroachment in this domain is directly proportional to the retreating spinelessness of the Quebec government. Quebec is still part of Confederation, as we were reminded by the elections of October 29, 1973. There exists a de facto relationship of complementarity between Quebec and the central government, even if Quebec's complementing of English Canada has been done with very little grace. French Canadians see themselves as necessary to English Canadians and, as it were, an integral part of their reality. The Québécois are as near as makes no difference to sticking their noses into English Canadians' business out of vindictive reciprocity, just as English Canadians interfere in our affairs.

The bond of complementarity between Quebec and Canada perhaps purges the French Canadian of some of the grudges he bears, but it also holds his thought in thrall to a disabling relativity. Moreover, since the central government, aided and abetted by Quebec, shows great concern for the preservation of French in Quebec, the French Canadian is given a feeling of security; he no longer fears the disappearance of French or its suppression in favour of English, and French acquires, under this double tutelage, the status of protected language.

Let us turn now to the question of immigrants. We have scruples about forcing immigrants to register their children in French schools, while hundreds and thousands of French Canadians have long been obliged to speak English and live in silence, such has been the pressure on them to express themselves only in a foreign language. And these French Canadians were not immigrants; they had not chosen to settle in another country—they were at home and in their own land. We have scruples about using the courts to make our country French again, when others have had no scruples about using force to anglicize it! That takes some beating!

Immigrants are potentially the most insidious aspect of our anglicization. It is no longer the English who want to assimilate us; it is the immigrants who not only want to be assimilated to the English, but who dispute our right to assimilate anyone at all to our culture and our language. They are not resisting us; they are disputing our right to pass legislation governing immigration to Quebec and, by so doing, are eroding our position more seriously than ever before in our past. And once assimilated, it will be no time at all before these immigrants themselves start assimilating others to English.

The linguistic situation in Quebec is being poisoned and infected by the immigrants. Tensions were starting to disappear between French and English Canadians; now they are reappearing and multiplying seriously between French Canadians and immigrants because the latter are in disdainful ignorance of the rights won by French Canadians. I almost believe that immigrants see French Canadians as immigrants—thereby ignoring a history they have never been taught—and that they aggressively refuse to be integrated in a group which is autonomous and likes to think of itself as sovereign.

In other words, by their attitude, immigrants show no respect for Confederation, which goes to show, in my opinion, that they came to settle not in Canada (the reality of which they refuse) but in a country which is merely the anteroom of the United States. At present, the immigrants are not only slowing Quebec's progress towards independence, they are also distorting the normal workings of Confederation. There is no xenophobia involved in obliging immigrants to demonstrate political loyalty and cultural consistency; the immigrants are the ones who would have to answer the charge of xenophobia, for they are the source of the cultural negativism which is so destructive to the Québécois community.

In this context, to dream of instituting a new language—*joual*—is to capitulate in advance by seeking refuge in an impregnable and indecipherable linguistic fortress.[2] The only way *joual* can be revolutionary is if Quebec remains colonized. For, after a successful national liberation, *joual* would have lost its revolutionary value and would be nothing more than a residual deformation of our dialect. A language cannot be founded on the necessarily temporary existence of a colonial regime; when the regime in question is overthrown, the language of resistance would become archaic and counter-revolutionary.

Joual is often presented as the painstaking phoneticization of a French that has been deliberately sacrificed. The action of phoneticizing everything creates the illusion of nationalizing French (which, by the way, was never imposed upon us). In reality, this is to deny both writing and printing; with a single gesture both consciousness and thought are dismissed with a wave of the hand. To phoneticize everything is to act as though the writer were unaware of the arbitrary nature of a language's system of spelling and of language in general. It is to act as though we were dealing with illiterates.

["Le *joual*-refuge." *Maintenant* 134 (March 1974): 18–21.]

Editor's Notes

1. Victor-Lévy Beaulieu is a prolific Quebec author and publisher.
2. The original text as published in *Maintenant* stopped here. The rest of the essay appeared for the first time in the version published in *Blocs erratiques*, pp. 137–42.

"The Disappearance in Language of the Poet"

(MALLARMÉ)

"The pure work implies the disappearance in language of the poet, who lets the words take control... "[1]

This text (which I have in my hands) was written to be read by its author. In that respect, at least, it differs from what is normally called literature. For in literature the text is written to be read by someone else and that someone else is the reader.

I think it is important to insist on the otherness of the reader, for it is the reader's alterity that attests to the fact that writing is a vector activity. The written word is always written for someone, for a collective persona, for a reader who is often unlikely and unpredictable. However senseless it may appear in certain respects, writing always has a point. It is aimed at a reader who is also a judge, who confers value on what he accepts and consigns to oblivion the things he rejects.

To have invented writing is all well and good, but to have in-

107

vented reading is the work of a madman! It has taken centuries for writers to become more afraid of being read than of writing. Yet we have come to that point. But enough of this truth and back to the text...

Writing is an inverted reading and reading an inverted writing. Therefore, writing is the inverse of passive reading, and reading the passive inverse of writing.

Writing: an inverted reading; which in practice means that I am preoccupied to the point of obsession with the reader. As I write, I imagine I am reading myself through the eyes of this stranger and I do not want the pleasure he takes in reading my text to be uniform, constant or, as it were, predictable; I want it to go through several levels of intensity, to be enriching and unpredictable, capable of surprising and even shaking him. When I am writing, I think of the reader as my other half, and I feel the need to find him and install him in my text. A total writing is one which is oriented entirely towards the possible reading it will receive. The writer's stylistic experiments, his figures, his special effects, his verbal strategies, these various aspects are all initially relational rather than expressive, for they depend on a projected relationship between author and reader.

Literature has two sides to it: an intentional side, which is the side of writing, and a surface side, which corresponds to reading. It sometimes happens in the study of literature (as, for example, in a certain kind of psycho-criticism) that the intentional side is examined in isolation, with regard only for the author; this results in the intentionality, the direction and destination of which are overlooked, becoming unintelligible.

The relation between writing and reading is fundamental to the phenomenon of literature. Writing is the negative which, when developed in the process of reading, prints an image in the consciousness. If there is no developer, the negative can never be printed; and if there is no negative to bring to life, the developer has nothing to develop.

The pull of any piece of writing towards its destination brings moral pressure to bear on the writer, making him tend to what Mallarmé calls "the omission of self" or, in a more winsome vein, "the disappearance in language of the poet." I am not offering a commentary on Mallarmé here; I am simply drawing on similarities of thought. I believe that writing has to purge itself drastically of the writer's ego. Unfortunately, writing has been the object of every egocentric investment imaginable, to the point where this cluttered, overloaded writing has finally replaced literature and has almost become an obstacle to communication, weighed down as it is with everything that has been deposited in it. The writer must be more self-sacrificing and see that writing is not an object in itself, that it has value only if it is effectively inverted by the act of reading. Writing never equals literature.

For some, writing is an outlet for the unconscious or a practical tool for introspection. But to me the benefits of this kind of writing seem very dubious in comparison with the techniques of introspection offered by psychology and its offshoots; similarly, its potential for expression seems questionable in relation to the other expressive arts, which are more spectacular and more generous. Writing has more of a communication function, which cannot be set aside. It conveys messages, articulating discourse so as to give it greater impact on a possible reader. It can express a vast range of moods and formulate ideas with precision, but in every case it communicates its affective and intellectual burden to a collective or individual addressee. When writing has done its job, it is transformed into reading. Literature is born, so to speak, from this union of writer and reader. At its best, this coming together has an element of love at first sight, a spectacular coupling which lasts as long as it takes to read the text. This act of union, which is at the origin of literature, takes on a sacred quality; it is the impulsion to joy, exaltation and thought itself.

The contingent, chance aspect of this event leads me to ponder certain questions—which I will take the liberty of bringing to your attention.

—What is a reader looking for when he picks up a novel or a series of novels?
—Do not television and cinema provide the same pleasures and emotions for less effort?
—From a different point of view, what then are the motives which lead certain people to write novels?
—Do the major innovations of literature operate on the level of writing? If so, do they have the effect of orienting the writing dynamically towards the reader or of magnifying, dislocating and overcoding it, thereby taking it further and further away from its destination?
—Is writing, once it has been transformed into unwriting, still an inverted reading? Is it not rather a show of pride on the part of a writer who is confined to the despair of his social isolation?

I have just outlined some of the avenues which are open to my personal exploration. The questions are sincere; I am not trying to hide my own uncertainties behind a mask of riddles.

The reader has no work. Not in the sense that he has nothing to do (although that, too, would be valid), but in the sense that he is waiting for someone to offer him *a work*. His having no work calls for a work. The worker and the person with no work thus find themselves in a situation where communication becomes possible through the medium of the book. Writer and reader commune with one another in and through reading, participating in a silent celebration which brings them together out of time. In this way, literature does not exist fully when the work is written, but only when a reader traces the words and sentences back to their source to become the work's co-creator.

The reader plays the part of officiating priest in this celebration; he officiates by reading the written text, by making it his own and giving it—in his own mind—a new meaning, a connotation and a dimension which are perhaps unique.

Each new reading of a book constitutes a new celebration and adds a little more value to the book; each new reading reflects, as it were, upon the work. This increase in value has nothing to do with the un-written precepts of commercial distribution; for publishers, I know, the books which sell well have greater value. But what I am trying to say here concerns the non-monetary value of those works which have attracted a large number of readers. In this respect, each new reading corroborates the work's powers of attraction. I am more and more convinced that works incorporate external time, inasmuch as those works which have successfully stood the test of time also turn out to be the richest and most valuable ones. That is perhaps a truism; but I had to arrive by myself at an appreciation of its full import.

The reading experience allows the reader to live a kind of condensed version of life. Within the confines of an imaginary order, at the heart of the book, the reader—whom I always imagine to be trembling—will experience catharsis. In the past, he would identify with heroes, getting inside their skin and living out their many adventures. Now that novels have abandoned their old objective narrative techniques to offer their own literary genesis in lieu of adventure, the reader transfers his emotional investment to book or author; he responds to the formal innovation of today's novels as though it were a test or trial of ancient times — something like the enigma of the Sphinx. If the novelist comes out of the ordeal triumphant, then the reader quite rightly shares in his victory since he has triumphed over the formal complexity of the work; the novelist's triumph is followed, like links in a chain, by the reader's. For writer and reader alike, formal complexity might therefore be regarded as an ordeal of the kind faced by the heroes of legend.

Reading does not stop when the book has been put down. It goes on after the last page is turned, prolonging at such moments the inward time of celebration.

Some closing thoughts:

I have found that, in contemporary books published in Quebec and elsewhere, the author's presence is all too noticeable. The book ends up being contaminated by the presence of its author, to the point where the whole activity of reading revolves around whether one loves or hates the author's actual person. I have come to the conclusion that what we need is to practice absence, so that books are not lost sight of by virtue of being mired in considerations such as these. I even go so far as to wonder whether the ultimate literary innovation would not be a return to anonymity: anonymous authors for anonymous readers.

It is quite possible that, because of my revolt against the exaggerated presence of writers, I shall be regarded as a ghost. How should I react to that? I realize that it is pretty hard to confine one's disappearance to the sphere of language. To disappear is to die a little. But it ill becomes me to die a little.

["'La disparition élocutoire du poète' (Mallarmé)."
Cul Q 4–5 (Summer-Autumn 1974): 6–9.][2]

Editor's Notes

1. The French text reads: "L'oeuvre pure implique la disparition élocutoire du poëte, qui cède l'initiative aux mots.... " It can be found in Mallarmé's *Oeuvres complètes* (Paris: Gallimard, Bibliothèque de la Pléiade, 1945), p. 366.
2. This essay was first given as a paper on 27 November 1973 at a conference on "Quebec Literature. Writing/Reading" ("Littérature québécoise. Écriture/lecture") held at the University of Quebec at Montreal (UQAM).

Why I Am Disenchanted with the Wonderful World of Roger Lemelin

Mr. Roger Lemelin
President and Publisher
La Presse

I firmly believe that frankness and respect for others are preferable to all the parades, all the bragging, all the strategic duplicities, all the tacit understandings (the principal advantage of which lies in the ambiguity of what is understood), all the swaggering, all the tipping of winks and the endless ploys to which you have subjected your public in order better to manipulate it and, if we are to call a spade a spade, in order to deceive the people with whom you come in contact.

Please believe me, Mr. Lemelin, when I say that if today I have come to the point where I find it necessary to start a letter in this fashion, it is because I am disenchanted with the "wonderful world of Roger Lemelin"! (The expression is yours.) One might have thought that this vast enterprise of speculation, unscrupulous dealing and throat-cutting would be the means to a vigorous, productive, healthy organization. Not so! With all the human, cultural and financial capital you control, you have no desire to create, but simply to rule. Under your influence, everything turns to stone. The court where you hold sway reminds me of a collection of zombies, summoned into existence and reduced, without even knowing what is happening to them, to a state of bureaucratic aphasia complete with car allowance and expense account.

What else is there to say, but that like a true prince you make paupers of those you take graciously under your wing; I suppose that daily repetition of such acts serves to sharpen your awareness of your wealth. For, when all is said and done, wealth can be measured only in relation to its absence amongst those one sees on a regular basis. Moreover, by constantly renewing your stock of servants, you have even found a way of avoiding the pitfalls associated with this little game. To put it bluntly, after two years in your entourage, just when they are starting to see through you, your minions find themselves escorted off the premises to make room for new and innocent blood.

Acting in strict accordance with the instructions you gave me when I was hired, I have done everything in my power since coming to Les Éditions La Presse to set up a real Quebec publishing house. (A Quebec version of the best French houses, was how you put it.[1]) In the process, I have encountered enormous resistance which, with the benefit of hindsight (and supporting documentation), I now see as so many obstacles you have strewn like flowers in my path. The list of large-scale Quebec publishing projects that have been contemptuously set aside by your proxies is impressive, at least inasmuch as Les Éditions La Presse have made considerable investments in and through me in these projects to which I have devoted my time and energy and which have been torpedoed at a rhythm just irregular enough for me not to realize right away that while you, Mr. Lemelin, were encouraging me over gourmet dinners to continue my efforts, you knew full well that your assistants, acting under your orders, would block them. Incredible but true! And it was not inevitable that I should see through your system, given the fact that I had a vested interest in taking good care of the man who had regally contrived to institute my financial dependence. But understand I did. Certain friends who have followed my progress these last few months know the crises I have gone through and the torments I have known. In this "wonderful world," Mr. Lemelin, everyone loses except you, for you never have to account for the human capital invested. The only thing that counts for you is the bottom line; according to your shameful philosophy, human capital is redeemable at any time and can therefore be reduced to its market value.

I denounce the influence you have on the culture of Quebec. It is destructive. You are colonizing us from within. Your dealings with Hachette[2] show the extent to which our status as a colonized people suits you. (Did you not declare, Mr. Lemelin, in the June 5, 1976 issue of *Perspectives:* "... I do not talk about 'our literature,' I talk about literature. There is no such thing as Quebec literature; there is only a North American literature in French.") When you deal in news and culture and are the head of an organization as vast and complex as La Presse and its affiliated companies, you are engaging in cultural destruction if you run your affairs with your usual easygoing charm, handing over the reins whenever you feel like it to a team composed of Guy Pépin, Guy Pépin and Guy Pépin, who, in a matter of months, has poisoned the atmosphere in your entourage. The journalists at La Presse would be surprised to find out (but then again, perhaps not) that even the news editors receive their orders from Guy Pépin and that, in spite of the compartmentalization that is there to protect freedom of information, Mr. Guy Pépin, the shadowy representative of Power Corporation, has precedence over everyone.

Will the real Mr. Lemelin please stand up! Caught between your authorized representative, Guy Pépin, and Paul Desmarais, the president of Power Corporation, who are you if not Paul Desmarais' puppet? It has taken me some time to come to this conclusion, but that is not surprising since for a long time I refused to see myself as the guarantee, in my own humble way, of Roger Lemelin's nationalist credentials. I thought you had too much integrity to use me like that. But now the truth is staring me everywhere in the face.

Let us put our cards on the table. Power Corporation has won right down the line by managing to keep me in the dark both as to the role I was to play at Les Éditions La Presse and as to the total freedom of Roger Lemelin, blinding me to the truth of his anti-Quebec machine fronted by two Quebec writers. The reality is quite different... and quite pathetic.

You have really shown yourself unworthy of your country, Mr.

Lemelin, in offering to dress up the whole operation in your Buckingham Palace style in exchange for a fat salary from Power Corporation.

Your obsession with money, Mr. Lemelin, has something pathological about it, for when it comes down to it you do not have the usual attributes of a real managing director. You run La Presse by a process of administrative improvisation, the immediate success of which masks a real squandering of the human and financial assets of the enterprise. All you see is the cash in hand. For you, capital is nothing more than the sum of liquid assets; the other assets of a business—complex, social, cumulative and untranslatable in terms of cash value—carry no weight with you; obsessed as you are with the tangible, monetary benefits to be had by cultivating the surface, you make no attempt to see beyond and deal rationally with the overall productivity of the total assets. You need to be reminded, Mr. Lemelin, that this money smacks of treason. I hasten to say, without raising my voice, that one can be a traitor to one's country even in times of peace. You have done much that is treasonable, Mr. Lemelin, even launching me on this anti-Quebec mission for the sole purpose of magnifying your treachery through my presence at your side.

And if people are taken aback by words like treason and treachery, I suggest they refer to the dialectic of traitor and patriot.

The kind of cultural colonization which you, Mr. Lemelin, practise, under the protection and for the profit of Power Corporation, deserves to be denounced. It has been my experience at Les Éditions La Presse that the more Quebec publishing tries to give itself a national identity, the greater the resistance it encounters. Anything which tends to place value on Quebec's standing as an independent political entity or a national culture—even on the level of scholarly works—has for some months now been brutally rejected by your delegates. And I know for a fact that their orders came from you. The text I am writing you today, Mr. Lemelin, is not so much a letter as an analysis of both a situation and a disturbing experience that I have lived through; an experience which was all the more painful for being accompanied by a realization that I had initially put off (much as one sets aside a prejudice) only to end up bowing to the facts and seeing the true nature of the moral minefield in which I find myself. Writing this letter to you, Mr. Lemelin, is a way of describing for you my progress towards the obvious, but if I make the letter public before you receive it yourself, it is to make clear why and in what sense I as an individual have walked into a trap which usually works on the collective level, and also to expose publicly what I have found out, in spite of the humiliation that such exposure may make me feel.

You are aware that, before resorting to an open letter, I have written untold letters and memos, made countless phone calls, in order to shed some light on the situation at Les Éditions La Presse and get the clean-up process started. You have remained cloistered in your power, not deigning even to discuss the problem, a fact which I find all the more senseless as it was you yourself who brought me to La Presse, propounding in the early months your precepts of openness, loyalty and sincerity in our relations. In conclusion, I should inform you that I am not resigning, because I consider it my duty to defend the values I believe in and to oppose your positions openly.

["Pourquoi je suis désenchanté du monde merveilleux de Roger Lemelin." *Le Devoir*, August 7, 1976, p. 5.]

Editor's Notes

1. The actual reference is to Gallimard's prestigious NRF imprimatur.
2. A French publishing house which does business in Canada.

The Text or the Surrounding Silence?

"All specialization has a diminishing effect" (T.W.)

Michèle,

I am anxious to deliver this text you asked me to write for *Mainmise*.[1] And I use the term *deliver* quite deliberately, even though my text is stillborn and all the king's horses and all the king's men... You have no idea.

In the beginning, I dreamed of producing a vast and fascinating gloss on world-weariness, but, though you don't notice it at the time, world-weariness makes shortcuts impossible and requires that we spell things out one at a time and at length in a manner which seems to me distinctly at odds with *Mainmise's* ideology. And after all, what a chore! Why expend so much digital energy writing about nothing but oneself? Why not relax and simply become other people? It would be so much

117

simpler, so much easier and—who knows?—maybe more uplifting. The exorbitant price of individuation can never be too loudly decried.

You have understood, or rather guessed, Michèle, that I wanted to situate my text within the problematics of the individual and the collective. Indeed, I dreamed of putting my thinking fingers on the join between self and nothingness and of charting the fluid frontier which separates self and other, the individual and his own intoxicating dissolution in the collective mind.

But suddenly I am struck by the analogy between this opposition of the ego and the infinite and the typographical contrast which sets the text against the silence of its margins, which surround and jostle it and will soon devour it. The text does not fill the page, any more than the human being occupies the fullness of his existential field. Think of the pressure of all that expanse that strangles every printed character, every word, every one of Musset's sobs, every interminable and divinely convoluted sentence that Proust ever wrote. When all is said and done and all things considered, being is defined by nothingness and not vice-versa. Life really only emerges from its absolute opposite. Nothingness creates distinctions, just as the margins invent the text.

Existence is an interpolation.

"I am not what I am" (O.S.)

> This last sentence, it has to be said, verges on murder, unless it hides one—the murder of the one by the many.

I leave so that I may find you again; I pretend to lose you so that I may reinvent you. Curtain.

Act Two. Yes, there is a sequel. And I was intending, Michèle, to attack the second part of my text by showing that the self is expanded by the collective, which transforms one's perception of reality. Put like that, it sounds simplistic, and yet the equation has to be reformulated an untold number of times before the mind really starts to grasp its staggering implications. Imagine some poor guy suddenly vested with the powers of the many: all at once his most pleasing sensations fade away, his original thoughts grow dull, his subtle tastes melt into thin air. Nothing left. A wisp of smoke disguised as a thinking reed. Tainted meat for vegetarians. For Christ's sake.

> Worse still, Michèle, imagine that the individual being never transcends chance, and that the aleatory entity which dominates and corrupts everything is number. Once again, it starts to look like the ubiquitous and all-seeing margin, which in the last analysis is the only discernible structure of any printed text. By virtue of being permeated by the margin which lies in wait for it, the written text no longer appears as an insert but as an excerpt. One can always decentre a little further to left or right, but if the text is ex-centration, it is attached only to its own margin.

The text is written continuously in the text or in the margins of another text. The self is an intertext, and consciousness of the self a chaotic commentary—marginalia which are sometimes imperceptible but always formative, always originating. The finite is delicately bounded by its own infinity; it is as though the darkening light of intelligence were enveloped in a luminous shadow.

> Sometimes silence is necessary, but I go on letting the superfluous words flow. Superfluity is the indelible sign of poverty and I feel inordinately poor.

What I wanted to tell you, when all is said and done, Michèle, is that individual history is inextricably bound up with the cosmic adventure and that the mystic sense slips in at the point of articulation between self and collective. The mutations of perception that can be attributed to the permeation of the self by the collective are nothing in comparison with the revolution brought about by the resurgence of the mystic in individual existence. St. Paul once said: "Happy the world which will end in ecstasy."[2]

> Between this Pauline notion of ecstasy and the extravagance of the contemporary idea of the ec-

static orgasm, the difference is one of intensity and not of kind. According to St. Paul, ecstasy is synonymous with gentleness; there is nothing less orgasmic than this joy which floods the being, nothing less like tripping out than this slow-motion journey to the nucleus of the self.

God alone is before us and around us. And, as Schiller said, "the middle is more consistent than the centres." There is no getting out, which is why I stay. I stay and wait for the end of an endless flight.

["Le texte ou le silence marginal."
Mainmise 64 (November 1976): 18–19.]

Editor's Notes

1. This letter was written to Michèle Favreau, one of the editors of *Mainmise*, in response to a request for an article made shortly after Aquin's break with Les Éditions La Presse. The title is not Aquin's but comes from the magazine.
2. The attribution would seem somewhat unlikely.